It's Not About Your
Money
It's About Your
Life

*Finding Clarity and Financial Confidence
for the Road Ahead*

Elfrena Foord, Carol Van Bruggen,
Chuck Ebersole, and Laura Harger Pajak

www.wealthandbeyondprogram.com

Cover design: Kelley Falk
Book design: Jack Steiner

First Edition

Printed in the United States

ISBN 978-1-4495932-2-3

Acknowledgments

All authors come to a book-writing project with life experiences. With that in mind, we appreciate the contributions our parents made to our lives to get us on the right path.

The four authors would like to thank those who helped with this book. Jennifer Summer-Tolman and Heather Estay helped in a significant manner, and without their input this book would not have happened. Our readers, Mark Sewell, Bob McLean, Beverly Jackson, Karen Kieweski, and Frank Glick, gave us invaluable feedback. Our editor, Jenny Govier with Colborne Communications in Toronto, was such a thorough and friendly person throughout the process—and, of course, through the magic of technology, we have not met. Thanks to John Gardiner for his illustrations. And thanks to Kelley Falk for not only reading the manuscript but designing the book cover.

All of us have benefited from Dan Sullivan and his Strategic Coach® program, which has helped us create and communicate our Wealth and Beyond Program®. The Legacy Companies, LLC and Todd and Scott Fithian have taught us many ideas that we use to help clients take action and achieve what's most important to them.

We thank our spouses, Bruce Hester, Steve Kuhn, Odette Ebersole, and Steve Pajak, for their encouragement and support of the book.

Most of all, we want to thank our clients, who have taught us the most and who have enriched our daily lives with the pleasure of working with them.

The Authors

Elfrena Foord, Carol Van Bruggen, Chuck Ebersole, and Laura Harger Pajak, all CERTIFIED FINANCIAL PLANNER™ practitioners, have been in business together in Sacramento, California, since 1986. Visit their website, www.wealthandbeyondprogram.com, for more information.

Table of Contents

PART **FOUR**: Contentment

Appendices

References and Resources

Introduction

It's Not About Your Money, It's About Your Life

This is not another financial planning book, nor is it a book of secrets to becoming wealthy, or a guide to managing your wealth once you get there. This is a travel guide, an affirmation, and a workbook for making the most of what you've diligently earned and saved. Throughout this book, we will help you look beyond your habitual expectations and get past the accumulate-and-protect mindset, as well as other limiting mindsets. We will inspire you to think about what is really important to you, and to use your wealth to achieve your goals in a logical and responsible, but liberating, manner.

However, we are financial advisors. The authors have decades of experience helping clients achieve financial independence and peace of mind. We help our clients realize their dreams not only by guiding them as they accumulate and manage wealth, but by helping them discover their unique visions, evaluate the changes they would need to make to attain their visions, and make their visions a reality. That's the key to the Wealth and Beyond Program®.

We developed the Wealth and Beyond Program® over a decade ago, and we've been using it since. The program starts by helping you clarify what is most important to you, then moves on to making that happen. You start your journey from a place of freedom and inspiration, not with numbers on a page. The numbers are important, of course, but when you let your imagination soar, you become inspired and energized, and the task of figuring out how the numbers will help your dreams come true becomes enjoyable and rewarding.

One of the biggest rewards of working through this process is confidence. You will gain confidence knowing that you have a clear vision for your future. You will gain confidence knowing that you have enough, or will have enough in time, to achieve your vision, and that you are working toward your future. Your next step will be to look at how you can make a contribution to your community and your family that will be meaningful and rewarding to you as well as to those who benefit from it. Finally, you will be content, knowing that everything is in order and the future is bright.

Throughout our 20 years in business, we have met many clients with unique problems, dreams, and outcomes. This book includes stories about people we know who painted a new picture of themselves and began to view their future differently, making sure to include all the values and goals that were most important to them. Through their stories, you'll learn about the blind spots that people frequently have when it comes to money. You may even see a bit of yourself in these stories. Many of the blind spots may sound familiar; many are deeply ingrained habits or beliefs that hold us back from realizing our true potential. We also hope these stories will show you the variety of solutions and opportunities that are available to you, and will inspire you to make your own dreams come true.

We can't guarantee the Wealth and Beyond approach will cause you to turn your whole life around, but it will encourage you to rethink your perception of money and free you to change how you make your decisions for the future. We sincerely hope it will guide you toward discovering what's important to you, and to knowing that you have *enough*.

PART **ONE**

Clarity

Paradigm Shift

It's not about your money, it's about your life: thinking along these lines represents a major paradigm shift for most people. An approach that starts by defining what's most important to you and focuses on the *treasures* of wealth (clarity, confidence, contribution, and contentment) is very different from one that focuses on money alone. The following historical example clearly illustrates this paradigm shift.

There was virtually no physical disease or psychological illness in Hawaii prior to the arrival of missionaries. Any problems were brought to a kahuna, one of the healers of the islands who practiced the ancient arts of Huna. A kahuna viewed symptoms holistically and worked with the patient to unearth their root cause. Once they determined the causes, the kahuna would insist that the patient commit to his or her own healing. To cure a fever, a patient might have to ask forgiveness for a past transgression or find a different occupation. The source of a stomachache might be an untruth that had to be exposed or an unresolved sadness requiring healing. Kahunas did not heal their patients, but guided and supported them on their path to healing.

Western medicine views illness quite differently, though many practitioners are now acknowledging the need for a holistic perspective. Physicians concentrate on curing physical symptoms that they assume come from physical causes. All physical bodies are assumed to operate the same way, so diagnostics are based on a one-size-fits-most logic. Specialists focus on specific parts of the body to the exclusion of others, and patients expect to be healed by a pill or surgical procedure or, even worse, an inconvenient change in lifestyle.

Could these two approaches to health be any further apart? Clearly, there are fundamental differences in these two paradigms. A perspective that focuses on wealth and money alone will treat the symptoms by devising financial tactics, will deal only with the physical—money and assets—and won't require your full participation. But when wealth's underlying treasures are the goal, the financial approach is much more like ancient Huna. It takes into account your life as a whole, your core values and aspirations, who you are now, and who you wish to become. It recognizes that your wealth is nothing in itself without the treasures it can offer.

CHAPTER ONE

Creating Wealth *versus* Creating Happiness

It is pretty hard to tell what does bring happiness; poverty and wealth have both failed.

KIN HUBBARD, CARTOONIST

When asked what would add to their happiness, most Americans automatically respond, "More money." They've been raised to believe that their happiness, their very self-worth, depends on how much money they make or the total value of their assets. Many of us, though, have a sneaking suspicion that something is missing in this equation.

Our suspicion is supported by research: in 1957, 35 percent of Americans surveyed claimed to be "very happy" with their lives. At that time, the average American earned $10,000 per year (adjusted for inflation) and lived without a dishwasher, clothes dryer, television, and air conditioning. In 2004, despite the fact that inflation-adjusted income had tripled and households boasted all sorts of amenities, only 34 percent said they were "very happy."[1] In another study, the American Amish, who live an antiquated, rural lifestyle with few luxuries, rated themselves 5.8 on a happiness scale of 1 to 7. Members of The Forbes 400 list, who have a minimum net worth of $125 million, took a similar survey and rated themselves *exactly the same.*[2]

Few would argue that poverty is the path to happiness. A study at Erasmus University in Rotterdam, Netherlands, supports the obvious conclusion that people who live in poverty are frustrated and stressed by their lack of resources.[3] Being able to meet basic survival needs is critical to a sense of well-being. Beyond that, however, the correlation between money and happiness gets fuzzy. A *Time* magazine poll showed that happiness increased with income up to the level of $50,000 per year[4] (the median annual income for U.S. households is $43,000[5]). Above that level, income did not have a dramatic effect on happiness.

A recent survey revealed that 19 percent of people whose net worth is at least $500,000 worry *constantly* about having enough money, and 33 percent of those who have a net worth of $10 million or more experience the same constant worries.[6] Another study, of those in the $5 million to $50 million bracket, found that just over one-third of respondents felt financially secure.[7] Clearly, having more money does not guarantee a greater sense of security, optimism, or happiness.

The facts seem counterintuitive. Shouldn't wealth bring some sense of peace? As we've seen in our research and experienced first hand with our own wealthiest clients, often it doesn't. Why not?

Money Can't Buy Happiness—Or Can It?

It's not money that buys freedom; it's attitude that buys freedom.
THAYER CHEATHAM WILLIS, WEALTH COUNSELOR

People who have amassed wealth haven't necessarily discovered its underlying treasures. These treasures are diverse, limitless, and unique to you. They are the results of your aspirations and goals, and they are waiting to be discovered. They are found in the clarity of knowing what is important to you, the confidence that you have enough money, the ability to contribute to the lives of others, and the feeling of contentment that comes with knowing all is well. When you focus on your wealth rather than wealth's precious treasures, however, you can feel unfulfilled, and financial contentment can remain elusive. Our clients Jack and Barbara are a good example.*

> The treasures of wealth are the results of your aspirations and goals, and they are waiting to be discovered.

A hardworking couple—Jack and Barbara—inherited a large amount of money from Jack's uncle. The couple, in their early forties, had two teenage children and very successful careers. Jack was CEO of a technology firm; Barbara was a partner in an engineering firm. Their vague plan was that, if the investments did well, they

---

* Throughout the book, our clients' names have been changed to protect their privacy, and some anecdotes are composites.

could both retire early, travel, take up hobbies, and complete projects they'd put off for years. We ran the numbers and devised an investment plan. And the money grew.

Over the years, Jack and Barbara returned to us with new ideas and desires. They wanted to build a beautiful new home to be closer to their offices. Later, they wanted to buy a vacation home and a boat so they could spend more time together. They asked us to invest their retirement funds, and asked about options for funding their children's college tuition. They decided to donate some money to a few charities and to Jack's alma mater. For each request, we ran the numbers and devised a plan. And the money grew.

However, one year when Jack and Barbara came in for their On-Track Monitor session, they looked weary and depressed. Jack looked particularly tired and older than his age. We asked what was wrong.

"Jack is very stressed about work and worried about money," Barbara explained.

"You have a great deal of money saved in your personal accounts and retirement funds," we pointed out. "We've run the numbers, and you'll still have plenty of money to be financially independent, leave money to the children, and even give money away. If Jack wants to keep working to get maximum retirement and health benefits, he can work part-time for the next couple of years." It was a solid plan, a perfect and easy solution, and we were certain that Jack and Barbara would be pleased and relieved.

But they were not pleased. "But what if the market drops? Or we have a big emergency? Or the children need financial help? When I look at what we have compared to all of our neighbors, I know we aren't as well off as they are," Jack insisted.

Less than a year later, Barbara called us to say that Jack's health was not good and she thought it was time to finally update that estate plan. We asked if Jack planned to retire.

"No, he has the opportunity to take his company public, and the potential for profit is huge. We decided he'll continue to work another couple of years," Barbara explained.

The money had grown. It had been over 15 years since Jack and Barbara had walked into our office with Jack's inheritance. Fifteen years of conscientious planning, careful saving and investing, and in-depth annual reviews. But for what? We wondered if Jack would still be alive when the next On-Track Monitor review came around.

Jack and Barbara are a perfect example of successful, intelligent people who had blind spots when they looked at their own situation. Their blind spots included

- getting wrapped up in the responsibilities of work and not seeing other options;
- having only a vague vision of what their life outside of work could be;
- comparing themselves to others rather than being aware of their own desires and goals;
- not making health a high priority; and
- letting worries about emergencies and market fluctuations stop them from enjoying their money.

Discovering Your Blind Spots

Blind spots are beliefs, feelings, and habits you have that prevent you from making choices that will help you realize your vision, dreams, and goals, perhaps even your mission in life. By definition, people cannot recognize their own blind spots—the fish, after all, asks, "What water?"—but everyone has them, and everyone's blind spots are unique. There are, however, some common categories.

- Misinformation or lack of information
  EXAMPLE: I can give unlimited amounts to other people with no tax consequences.
- Irrational fears
  EXAMPLE: I don't trust anyone, so I'll keep my money under my mattress.
- Irrational optimism
  EXAMPLE: Technology stocks will continue to appreciate forever, so I'll plan to get a return of 20 percent on my investments in retirement.
- Feelings based on experiences
  EXAMPLE: My father went bankrupt owning a business, so I'll never own one, even though I'd like to.

- Beliefs learned as a child
  EXAMPLE: I must be frugal and always save some of my income, even when I am financially independent.
- Stubborn habits or behavioral patterns
  EXAMPLE: I'm a workaholic, so I don't want to stop working to enjoy the money I've earned.

The important question is how detrimental your blind spots are to your quality of life and financial well-being. If the impact of your blind spots is substantial or is affecting your happiness and the decisions you make, then you need to discover what they are and why you have them. A workaholic, for example, may have fears that keep him at work 75 hours a week and always connected to a laptop or cell phone. Of what is he actually afraid? He may be afraid of being broke or bored. He may avoid taking time off. He may fear that he will become an alcoholic like his father, or he may not enjoy spending time with his family. It is important to determine the root of your beliefs and behaviors.

Blind spots are hard to identify. With an extraordinary amount of introspection, focus, commitment, and intelligence, you might be able to discover what they are. But most people need help from an outside observer or advisor who can see what they cannot. If you want to discover how your money can bring you more fulfillment and satisfaction, you need to talk to someone who can explore your vision, values, and goals with you and see how you stop yourself from achieving them. You could talk to people with whom you have close personal relationships, such as your spouse, a relative, a good friend, or a business partner— someone who probably knows you better in some ways than you know yourself. Some people find that using an outside advisor is more comfortable. You may already have an existing advisor who is a good counselor and listener, or you could look for someone who specializes in life coaching, such as a wealth coach who integrates life goals and money.

The sad story of Jack and Barbara was the wake-up call that we, as a financial advisory firm, needed to create a new way of thinking that would help our clients learn to enjoy their money instead of being enslaved by it.

We found that this new approach, which we call the Wealth and Beyond Program®, was particularly valuable to the following types of people:

- The conscientious saver and investor who is afraid to spend any of the wealth she has amassed
- The wealth holders who are terrified of an economic downturn and don't believe they have the money they need to live the life they want, when they actually do
- The corporate executive who has reached all of his career and financial goals, and now feels that life has no purpose or zest
- The entrepreneurs, investors, professionals, businesspeople, and inheritors who never achieve that satisfying feeling that "enough is enough," and never learn to truly enjoy the wealth they have

There *is* a way to move beyond the mental traps of Jack and Barbara. We believe everyone has a choice when it comes to wealth, particularly when you could focus on the treasures of wealth and what they can do for you instead of focusing only on the wealth itself. Which choice do you think would bring you the most happiness?

Is wealth the goal, or is my wealth a vehicle for improving the quality of my life?

Is wealth a worrisome responsibility, or is my wealth a launching pad to new visions and possibilities?

Is wealth a source of insecurity, or is my wealth the foundation for the many choices available to me?

An Attitude Adjustment

What if all you needed to experience more happiness with your money was an attitude adjustment? Here's the good news: based on our experiences working with our clients, we can tell you that an attitude adjustment *is* all that's needed. Here's the not-so-good news: the adjustments required are not small. For some, the shift in thinking is huge. It requires you to be more open-minded, creative, and experimental. This may not feel comfortable and will be difficult for some people.

However, wouldn't the effort be worth it if it meant you could experience clarity, confidence, and contentment, all the while making valuable contributions using your wealth? Wouldn't it be worth it if you could join the 34 percent of Americans who consider themselves "very happy" and the 35 percent who report *no* concerns about money?

Experiencing happiness with your money requires you to be open-minded, creative, and experimental.

The principles that make sense when you focus on wealth's treasures may run counter to the basic financial beliefs you've held since childhood, many of which have been passed to you through several generations. We're going to tackle these discrepancies head-on, because the misconceptions many people hold about money are precisely what keep them from the satisfaction and fulfillment that wealth can bring.

The following are four examples of basic financial beliefs that trap people, versus principles that could help them enjoy the treasures of wealth.

I Need to Keep My Investments Growing versus It's Time to Start Spending What I've Accumulated

The latter assumption can't be right, can it? After decades of sacrificing for your future, you should squander all that you've accumulated and *spend* it?

For many people, it's hard to flip that switch. They've invested so much in preparing for the future that, now that the future is here, they still feel that they need to prepare.

The future has arrived. You have the money you intended to have. You are financially able to support a new vision, if you allow yourself to recognize it. What you may not have yet is a clear sense of that next vision. In later chapters, we'll talk about clarifying that vision and becoming confident in your financial capability.

Whoever Has the Most Toys Wins versus Whoever Lives the Life They Choose Wins

Because people are rarely encouraged to figure out what they really want out of life, they tend to look around at what others seem to want, and then want that for themselves. The problem is that what others want never feels satisfying.

Clare Boothe Luce's life illustrates this point. She married Henry Luce, editor of *Time, Fortune, Life*, and *Sports Illustrated* magazines. By all accounts, they had a wonderful, exciting life. She traveled the world as a war correspondent, was a U.S. congresswoman for two terms, and was appointed ambassador to Italy. By anyone's standards, she was highly successful. However, at the end of her life, she said she wished she had simply continued to write screenplays because that's what she really loved doing.[8]

Most people have forgotten what they really want, or even how to ask themselves the question, "What do I really want?" As kids, you easily and confidently told grown-ups what you wanted to be when you grew up. But sometime in your twenties, you may have abandoned what you wanted for what seemed acceptable or practical. In Chapter Three, we'll explore how to uncover your true desires once again.

There's Always a Risk that it Won't Be Enough Money versus There Is Enough After All

We have known many wealthy clients who were as compulsive about growing their wealth as people with anorexia are about losing weight. Long after we could see that they had plenty of money to sustain their families and their lifestyles, they felt they were lacking. They couldn't seem to turn off or redirect the intensity and drive they used when building their wealth. They compared their holdings with others who had more, and they pressured themselves to catch up. Though the original goal of building wealth for security and happiness was healthy, these clients were caught in an unhealthy cycle of "it's *never* enough."

How do you know when your pursuit of wealth has become unhealthy? See if any of these points apply to you:

- You often have feelings of anxiety and desperation about money.
- Each time you hit a financial goal, you feel that it is inadequate and set the bar higher.
- Your financial advisors tell you that you have plenty of resources to maintain your lifestyle for decades to come—but you can't quite believe them.
- You no longer enjoy the activity that built your wealth, but you feel that you have no option but to continue.

- Everyone around you wants you to slow down, yet you feel compelled to push as hard as you've always pushed, often ignoring signs of ill health or stress.

In Chapter Four, we'll discuss both the analytical and emotional components of *enough*.

Start with Numbers versus *Start with a Vision*

> *The only way of discovering the limits of the possible is to venture a little way past them into the impossible.*
> ARTHUR C. CLARKE, SCIENCE FICTION AUTHOR

For many people, a 20-mile hike would be a significant undertaking. What happens when you just examine the numbers? *I'm 55 and out of shape. The longest hike I've done was 10 miles. A 20-mile hike will take at least seven or eight hours. The temperature is supposed to be in the thirties by sundown.* Soon the adventure seems pretty daunting and not all that attractive. The numbers may persuade you not to attempt it.

But what if you started with the vision instead? *The scenery will be spectacular. The spring flowers will be in bloom, popping through the leftover snow. We'll have such a great time, talking and laughing, enjoying the peace and quiet. I'll feel so proud of myself to have done something I've never done before. It will be exciting to introduce my spouse to the park I used to love as a kid.* Suddenly the adventure seems exciting again. The numbers are something to consider, but not the main factor in your decision to go on this journey. Your vision, in some cases, may be so strong that it becomes your mission in life.

Should the numbers of your current finances be the main factor in determining your life journey, or should the main factor be the vision you have for your life?

A change in attitude is important, but it is also crucial to recognize that the financial advisory world can also keep you trapped in the old ways of approaching money management. We will deal with that obstacle next.

CHAPTER TWO

Traditional Approaches *versus* the Wealth and Beyond Approach

The only thing wealth does for some people is to make them worry about losing it.
ANTOINE DE RIVAROL, WRITER

Traditional approaches are based on getting reliable information or expert advice and using it to determine the best answers to your problems. In our complex, information-rich society, there are so many things to learn, and so many good answers to any problem. Listen to any radio talk show, and the host will have answers—good, smart answers that many people listen to, embrace, and benefit from. These listeners feel a sense of comfort because they believe this expert can help them. Visit any advisor's office—lawyer, accountant, investment professional, or insurance professional—and they will provide good advice and answers to your problems. These are smart people with experience, but they operate on several flawed premises.

One Size Fits Most

Radio talk shows definitely fit this category. How could they possibly cater to the individual situations of thousands of listeners? Many radio listeners have visited our offices and asked if mutual fund X is good for them. Occasionally, the answer is "Yes," but more times than not, the fund does not fit their unique situation. They would be unlikely to learn this from a talk show.

My Expertise Is Right for Your Problem

Many professionals only offer a fairly narrow band of solutions. One of our clients came in and announced that his father had transferred his house to our client and his sister based upon the advice of an expert on Medicaid planning. His father believed that, by doing this, if he needed to go on assistance, his children would still get an inheritance. However, there were two problems with this strategy. First, the father had enough money that it was unlikely that he would ever need to go on assistance. Second, they were creating a tax prblem for themselves. Two rules apply here: (1) When children are gifted an asset, they assume the cost basis (original cost plus any capital improvements) of the person giving it to them; and (2) when someone dies, their asset values step up to the fair market value at the date of death. So gifting the house meant the children would have more capital gains and pay more taxes when they sold it than they would if they inherited the house after the father died and kept the house in his name, when only the step up to fair market value would apply.

My Product Will Fix Your Problem

Many advisors are really salespeople in search of a sale, not advisors in search of the best solution for you. They will try to convince you that their product is the answer for you. This may or may not be true of your situation. Also, most advisors have a specific area of expertise. If your problem is in their area, you will get good advice. But getting a more comprehensive view of your situation takes time and more expertise than one person can provide. That is why we consider it so important that you discern for yourself what is most important and have a clear vision of your life, your values, and your goals so you can communicate them to the people you ask for advice.

When people search for answers and information on specific problems, they often end up with many solutions. This is called "piecemeal planning." Over the years we have seen many people who have implemented specific solutions for specific problems, but these solutions were not part of a holistic, integrated plan that produces the big-picture results they want.

Traditional planning focuses on what you have and how much you have. You're taught to work hard, save, invest, and protect the tangible assets that you've accumulated. You're instructed to hire competent advisors to assist you along the way—an attorney, an accountant, a few investment advisors, an insurance broker, and maybe others. For the most part, people become good stewards, follow the guidance of these advisors, and end up with the prize: a substantial portfolio.

That's the American dream, right? Make enough money and all will be well. But as we discussed previously, it's not always a dream come true. Like some physicians practicing Western medicine, many financial planners have been trained to look exclusively at your financial picture, not holistically at your life and your desires. Because the treasures of wealth aren't captured in traditional planning, the process may leave you uneasy, and there are specific reasons why.

Traditional planning doesn't take you beyond worry. Many people end up with financial pictures that are so complex they're not quite sure how all of the structures and investments fit together. Most leave with nagging concerns, wondering whether their parents are cared for, considering the ramifications of a business partner's death, or worrying about the instability of their career—all issues that their overall financial picture doesn't address. Some fear that their assets will completely dissipate if they don't stay right on top of them at all times. Whatever you fear, your problems and anxiety about money won't necessarily disappear as your portfolio grows. Here is what some of our wealthiest clients tell us when they first come to us:

> *I feel trapped by the responsibilities of money.*
>
> *My financial affairs are so complex that it's too much to handle. I wish it were simpler.*
>
> *I worry about all kinds of things, like, "What if I need long-term care down the road? What if the real estate market goes south? How will I pay for the roof that needs replacing in a few years? I have assets, but what about cash flow?"*
>
> *I should handle my financial affairs myself. I'd feel like a failure if I didn't, because I should be able to do this.*
>
> *I'm uncomfortable having anyone know my total financial picture and how much I really have.*

In Chapters Three through Seven, we'll talk about approaches that will help you gain clarity and confidence about your wealth and your financial decisions. It is crucial that you have a clear, ever-evolving picture of which financial instruments you have in place, why you have them, and what still needs to be done to make sure your financial picture is really complete. This approach ensures that all of your concerns are exposed and addressed. Finally, you'll be able to say:

Money has fallen into the background of my life and is no longer a concern.

I feel confident that I have a reliable team and effective systems in place that are right for me and the life I want.

I know that I have sufficient reserves to handle any unexpected expense or emergency.

I have enough liquidity and flexibility to handle market downturns or financial setbacks.

I know that money is a tool I can use to enhance my life.

I am clear about my cash flow needs and where that cash flow will come from.

Traditional planning never takes you beyond scarcity. Many people have been in earning and accumulating mode for so long that they can't seem to stop. They continue to focus on, or even obsess about, building their assets to respond to a vague internal uneasiness that says, "I need to keep building security for the future." Though they seem to have accumulated a lot, they never feel that it is enough. Rather than endowing them with a satisfying sense of abundance, their wealth leaves them wondering if what they have is sufficient. Worst of all, they don't even know how to go about figuring that out. Here's how the sense of scarcity is often expressed:

I've become so good at being thrifty and saving money that I can't seem to break the habit.

The financial projections show I have enough, but I just don't feel like I do. What proof do I have? I'd better build a little more just in case something unexpected happens.

I compare myself to people who have "real money" and I'm just not there yet. That makes me feel inadequate.

My business wouldn't survive without me. I'm burned out, but everything will fall apart if I don't stay at the helm.

It *is* possible to feel content with your finances, but you first must clearly identify what financial freedom means for you based on your core values, goals, and desires. Only then can you fully comprehend your unique personal financial independence number and know where you are in relation to it at any point in time. Even if you haven't achieved your financial goals, you'll be able to develop a clear path toward them. Then you'll be able to say the following:

> *I know that I don't need more money to be happy, and I know more money won't solve all of my problems.*
>
> *I am clear about the costs of my lifestyle and I know that my cash flow is sufficient, even abundant.*
>
> *I don't let fear of paying more taxes or dipping into assets stop me from having the cash flow that is important to me.*
>
> *I feel like sharing any surplus cash flow I may have with my family, friends, and community.*
>
> *I no longer compare myself to others, whether they are better off or worse off than I am. I don't let others' goals determine mine.*

Putting Clarity in the Driver's Seat

Traditional financial planning is not inadequate because its practitioners are incompetent. On the contrary, many professionals in the field are highly skilled and very sincere. Most stay informed in order to offer their clients the most sophisticated tools and strategies available, and many are extremely successful at helping their clients build wealth and substantially increase their net worth. However, as we saw with Jack and Barbara, it's not about the *money*— it's about attaining the life and the treasures you desire from your wealth. It's about the things you'd like to do or be or have; the cherished dreams for yourself, your family, and your community; the adventures you'd like to continue; the concerns or fears you'd like to address; and the legacy you would like to leave. *These are the things that should guide your planning processes.*

But in traditional planning, they usually don't.

However, they do guide the Wealth and Beyond approach. We suggest you start by finding clarity—identify your unique vision and the treasures you seek. Without absolute clarity about your ultimate destination, how can you possibly make good decisions on your journey?

Horizon First—Solutions Later

We believe that it is imperative to start your planning in a different place. It's not about a list of problems in search of solutions. When you are clear about your values and goals, you'll realize that it's all about the exciting vision that calls to you, the ultimate destination that inspires you, and the limitless horizon that is actually available to you. The Wealth and Beyond approach is a planning process that emphasizes the treasures of wealth. Rather than focusing on solving particular financial problems or achieving strictly financial goals, this approach begins above the horizon, by discovering your life goals. Only after that process is complete should you go below the planning horizon to choose the specific strategies, tactics, and tools that will help you realize your vision and that are compatible with your core values. This is the power of clarity.

Planning Horizon*

Your Vision, Values, and Goals
What They Are
Why They Are Important to You

PLANNING
HORIZON

YOUR FUTURE!

ABOVE THE LINE

BELOW THE LINE

Your Specific Strategies and Tools
How You Will Achieve Your Goals

---

* Planning Horizon is a trademark and copyright owned by The Legacy Companies, LLC. All rights reserved. Used with written permission. www.legacyboston.com.

Clarity

Clarity (n): order, certainty of mind; alignment with purpose, idea, or vision; unquestioned knowledge or insight

Finding clarity is the critical first step that will help you make a paradigm shift from traditional planning and wealth management approaches.

When we talk about clarity in the context of wealth's treasures, we are really talking about your vision, your core values, your aspirations, the fears or concerns you wish to resolve, and the goals you have for your life and your family. This is your ultimate destination, the reason you undertook the journey in the first place.

Finding clarity is the critical first step in making a paradigm shift from traditional planning and wealth management approaches.

Next, we show you specific ways to achieve this clarity. First, we will guide you through a five-step process that will build the confidence that so few people possess today.

PART **TWO**

Confidence

The Wealth and Beyond Approach

Confidence (n): sureness, self-assurance, poise, assurance, self-reliance, buoyancy, coolness; certainty, conviction, belief, faith, trust, support

Confidence is knowing where you are, where you are going, and how you will get there. When you are confident, you are calm and resolute.

The Battle of Midway was one of the most significant turning points in the Pacific Ocean theater during World War II. Exactly six months after the attack on Pearl Harbor, this conflict pitted a strong and highly successful Japanese Imperial Navy against a severely weakened United States naval fleet. Japan's plan was to lure America's few remaining carriers into a trap and sink them, occupy Midway Island to extend its defensive perimeter and prepare for future attacks against Fiji and Samoa, and, ultimately, invade Hawaii.

Despite the undeniable superiority of the Japanese Navy, the out-gunned United States Navy was victorious after three days of battle. Why? Because of the powerful, detailed information Allied intelligence services had gathered.

In a joint effort, British and American cryptanalysts had broken the code used by the Japanese military. These intelligence units were able to alert the U.S. Naval Command that an attack would begin on either June 4 or 5, 1942, and that Midway Island was the target. They were even able to provide a complete Japanese Imperial Navy battle plan. Because of this detailed and up-to-date information, the American forces entered the battle with a clear picture of where, when, and in what strength the Japanese fleet would appear, allowing them to deploy their limited resources to achieve the greatest effect. It also gave fleet commanders a clear basis upon which to make crucial decisions and take calculated risks during the battle itself.

Japan's information, on the other hand, was sketchy and limited, and the Japanese remained in the dark even after the battle had begun. The Imperial Navy had erroneously calculated that two heavily damaged U.S. carriers could not be repaired and battle-ready by that date. They had been told that the U.S. had been completely demoralized by Pearl Harbor and would avoid direct engagement with the much stronger Japanese fleet. Therefore, the Japanese Imperial Navy chose a doomed strategy of deception: luring the American forces to the area by widely dispersing the Imperial fleet, and creating the illusion that Japanese strength was minimal. During the operation itself, bad timing, misdirected resources, and difficult weather conditions also led to vague and inaccurate information about the movements of American forces. The ensuing confusion resulted in poor and delayed decisions that ultimately cost Japan its supremacy in the Pacific.

Which would you have preferred in that situation: to have superior forces with inaccurate and erroneous information, or to enter the battle with fewer resources but clear information about your enemy's movements and intentions? Which is the more powerful position? You may not have all the resources you'll need to fulfill your mission yet, but if you have clear information, you'll be able to make good decisions, choose successful strategies, and feel completely confident.

Though managing wealth should never feel like going into battle, you should feel totally confident with your wealth. It's one of the treasures of wealth that you deserve. To be confident, you need to be excruciatingly clear about where you want to be and where you are financially right now. You should have accurate, meaningful, and "decoded" information about your current and evolving financial position upon which to base your strategies. By having a strategy in place that helps you achieve what you really want from your wealth, you can feel confident that you are on the right track and will truly have *enough*.

CHAPTER THREE

Step One—
The Discovery Process

When you discover your mission, you will feel its demand. It will fill you with enthusiasm and a burning desire to get to work on it.

W. CLEMENT STONE, BUSINESSMAN AND AUTHOR

How will you discover your mission, your vision, and your core values, those attributes that can guide you to obtaining the treasures of your wealth? Maybe it's been awhile since you've stopped to ask yourself what's really important to you. To arrive at meaningful answers, the trick is to expand your thinking from "This is the way it is and the way it's always been" to "This is what is possible."

What is your vision, your unique reason for building wealth? The objective of wealth building is rarely wealth itself. You probably didn't carefully plan your future or work those extra hours just to see additional zeros in your bank balance (although that may have helped motivate you). Though you may have enjoyed the challenge of building your wealth, your ultimate destination doesn't have to be a number. The treasures of wealth are an important part of your challenge. Once identified, those treasures can become your purpose in life or your mission, and your wealth can support what is most important to you.

Your wealth should support your mission, your vision, your dreams, and your goals.

If you're like most people, as the years have gone by, you've become a little fuzzy about the concept of wealth as the means to an end. You have a vague notion of wanting security and freedom to accomplish your dreams, but you may have forgotten or abandoned that vision you had all those years ago. Sadly, many people only figure out their real purpose for building wealth when time has run out and it's too late. At that point, they become painfully aware of what they really wanted and are haunted by their regrets. One of our clients provides a poignant example of gaining clarity through regret.

A few years back, John sat by the bed of his dying wife as she told him of the many things she had always wanted to do but had not done: trips, adventures, special times with grandchildren.

With grief in his voice, John asked, "Why didn't you ever tell me this?" For years, this couple had enough resources to have and do all of the things they desired. But they were so immersed in the process of building wealth—of watching their feet as they walked the path—that they never talked about these possibilities until it was too late.

Now, Not Later

You're probably familiar with stories like John's; they are all too common. The purpose of a discovery process—the important first step in the Wealth and Beyond approach—is to examine yourself and question your reasons for building wealth. The process unearths your unique vision—your dreams, passions, and desires—so you can experience them during your life. Once you begin the process of working toward your vision, you may find that it is so important to you that it becomes your mission in life. An in-depth discovery process helps you define financial independence on *your* terms. This clear vision will guide all your financial decisions and strategies and will help you determine what resources you need to have in place.

Our client Sheila experienced the value of developing her vision after receiving a large bonus. A hard worker and determined goal setter, Sheila had started working at her company as a mailroom clerk, and 26 years later, she became CEO. Her career was all consuming, so her finances were not well organized. Still, Sheila had amassed several million dollars by the time she came to see us.

Initially, Sheila simply wanted a recommendation of where to stash her bonus, which would only have added to the hodge-podge of her portfolio. But through the discovery process, Sheila developed a broader vision for the ultimate purpose of her wealth. She began looking at her future with new eyes, uncovering exciting possibilities. Travel with her nephews? A second home in Europe? She loved her work, but realized that she could now enjoy a more flexible schedule and mentor others in the process. She also realized that she could take some of her business skills and apply them to causes that she held dear. Suddenly, Sheila's bonus was not just another page in her portfolio, but an entire world opening before her.

Sheila's Blind Spot: As a determined goal-setter, Sheila got stuck in the habit of saving everything she earned rather than balancing saving money for the future with enjoying some of her money today.

It's not about waiting until you have so much excess wealth that you can do everything you've ever wanted to do. If you wait until then, life may simply pass you by. Instead, we encourage you to explore what is important to you—and what isn't—on a regular basis. What things or activities are important right now? Are there better, more satisfying uses for your money?

Sam and Patty had always owned boats. Sam had been a sailor as a young man, and with boat docks practically at their back door, it seemed natural to them to own a boat. Each year, they purchased a new boat, turning in the prior year's model, and their boats grew in size. They loved and enjoyed these boats, and the year they came in to see us, they had just purchased a beautiful 55-foot motor yacht.

> If you delay enjoying your wealth until you have more than you need, life may pass you by.

At that point, however, Sam and Patty were doing less and less boating, and they had a strong desire to buy a vacation home in Hawaii. They also wanted to travel more, and give time and money to several causes that were important to them. They had experienced the truth in the old adage, "Boats are holes in the water into which you pour money." Because of their new desires, they decided to sell the yacht and purchase a much smaller boat that required less maintenance. This decision not only released funds to purchase the vacation home and to travel, but it also alleviated their guilt about not using the boat as often as they felt they should.

Sam and Patty's Blind Spot: Sam and Patty had always owned boats, but that didn't mean their interests wouldn't change over time. Changes like these can go unrecognized without a process to unearth new thoughts and feelings.

The Power of Your Vision

Holding a clear vision of what you want, whether for now or for the future, can be very powerful. Often, desires you feel intensely about and that you write down can take shape sooner than planned.

For years, Tim and Rachel talked about starting a business based on an idea Tim had. The business would take in donated cars and boats for non-profit organizations. Tim and Rachel would appraise the vehicle or boat, then fix it up or sell it for parts. The business would keep a percentage of sales proceeds and the rest would go to the cause designated by the donor.

Tim had worked for a government agency for many years and was in an upper management position, with years of pension money accrued. Although Tim was good at his job, he was passionate about his vision for their new business. Both he and Rachel saw its potential for growth and felt that in time it might earn them enough money to support another dream: to travel to exotic places. To get the new business off the ground, Tim wanted to cut back his hours at work, but stay in his position long enough to assure maximum retirement benefits. We helped them run the numbers for this plan, and they began their new venture.

Their original plan was to work at this business part-time for five to seven years, at which point Tom would retire from his government position, and they would work the new business full-time for another ten years. In less than two years, the new business was booming and making much more money than anticipated. Should they stick with the original plan and wait for the guaranteed higher retirement income, or focus full-time now to increase the size of the business? Tim decided to quit his job and focus on his fun, successful business, which continued to grow rapidly.

Tim and Rachel received an unexpected bonus. Because they did so much radio advertising, stations across the country gave them free incentive trips to places around the world. They received enough of these free trips that they were able to offer them to employees as well.

The moral of the story? The more detailed and elaborate your vision, the more likely it is to become your mission and, ultimately, your reality—often more quickly than you ever thought possible.

Discovery for Couples

What we must try to be, of course, is ourselves and wholeheartedly. We must find out what we really are and what we really want.

NELSON BOSWELL, MOTIVATIONAL AUTHOR AND SPEAKER

An in-depth discovery process is particularly important for couples. Too often, people do not discuss their underlying attitudes or most fervent dreams with their life partner. Although you are in the same boat, you may be paddling in different directions without being aware of it. By sharing the discovery process with one another, couples can create joint plans and futures that satisfy both individuals.

> Our clients Jack and Tammy found this to be true. Jack had started with next to nothing and had worked hard to build a sizeable business. He and Tammy adored their family, but while Tammy wanted to give their children and grandchildren things that she and Jack never had growing up, Jack felt strongly that the kids needed to earn these things themselves to become as self-reliant as he was. Both perspectives are valid.
>
> Working through the discovery process, Jack and Tammy discussed their feelings about sharing their wealth with the family. The result was a compromise that fulfilled their contradictory desires: they figured out a way to provide their children and grandchildren with educational opportunities and even some luxuries in a way that fostered growth and self-reliance. They set up a donor-advised endowment fund so their children could give away its income to charities of their choosing, which would teach them the importance of being involved in their communities and the rewards of compassionate giving. They balanced providing for their children and sharing with others.
>
> This issue could have become divisive, but by delving into the discovery process and designing a plan that was fun and satisfying for both of them, they became a stronger team.
>
> **Jack and Tammy's Blind Spot:** Jack and Tammy saw the issue in black and white only—you either spoil kids or make them earn what they want. They learned through the discovery process that there are many ways to help children without spoiling them.

Your Vision Is Unique

How do you know when you've developed ideas that reflect your real desires? You'll smile, you'll feel excited, and you'll feel the desire to start working on them right away. If you don't feel any of those things, you haven't hit upon your personal vision yet. Here's the trap: too often, you've been programmed to want what you think you're supposed to want, or what others seem to want. If you've picked a destination that doesn't make you smile, doesn't inspire you, and doesn't make you feel more alive, you might be envisioning a destination that is not yours.

A business owner and his wife, Mike and Teresa, came to us to discuss the possibility of a second home in the wine country of Napa Valley. They loved the area; Mike's friends all had second homes, and his CPA told him it would be a great tax write-off. As we got into the discovery process and asked the question, "What is important about money to you?" their answers led in a different direction.

"It's all about freedom," Mike said. "I hate the idea of being tied down. I love the variety of activities that having my own business has allowed me to experience."

"And we both love to travel to new places and explore different cultures," Teresa added. "It fuels our creativity and makes us feel alive and vibrant." Based on that vision, the idea of using all of their discretionary income for a second home and being tied to the responsibilities of maintaining it didn't seem like such a great idea after all.

Mike and Teresa's Blind Spot: Purchases often come with a price beyond what you pay for them. Mike and Teresa did not realize that the financial obligation of a second home would restrict their freedom.

A clear vision also helps you make decisions that are intelligent and meaningful, as our clients Ann and John discovered.

With children grown and gone, and having a comfortable lifestyle, Ann and John were fairly free of stress. Their one cause of disagreement was the cabin that had been in John's family for generations. Though John felt obligated to keep the property in the family, none of the family members really enjoyed spending time there. Ann and John's passion, shared by their children and grandchildren, was to travel the world and explore exotic locations. The cabin sat unused year after year.

During the in-depth discussions of the discovery process, this issue came up. Ann and John realized that going on sports adventure trips was important to their values and part of the legacy they wanted to pass on to their children and grandchildren. Together, Ann and John finally decided that it would be okay to sell the cabin, but they would do it in a way that honored John's great-grandparents. They invited extended family for one last celebration at the cabin, and created a video of the cabin itself so future generations could see where their ancestors had homesteaded. This decision, once impossible to make, came from the clarity of Ann and John's vision for themselves and their family. They were able to feel completely at peace with the choice they made.

Ann and John's Blind Spot: Ann and John had not realized that sentimentality can get in the way of a family's true needs and wants.

Discovering Your Legacy

The future starts today, not tomorrow.

Pope John Paul II

Though our generation will live much longer than past generations, it's still true that none of us will make it out of here alive! So along with the vision of what you want to accomplish *during* your lifetime, we invite you to look at what you might accomplish *after* your lifetime. (We will discuss this further in Chapter Eight.)

Typically, estate planning addresses the money or tangible assets you intend to leave behind when you die. Focusing on the treasures of wealth gives you a different view of estate planning. What is the legacy you want to leave? Can some of that legacy be given during your lifetime?

If you start thinking beyond the notion of merely leaving money, your legacy can include experiences, opportunities, memories, and values. It could be traveling the world with your grandchildren to give them the opportunity to learn about other cultures. It could be opening your vacation cabin to at-risk children so that they can experience the great outdoors. It could be leaving your prize-winning quilts to a folk arts historical society, recording your family history for great-grandchildren, funding a small publishing venture for local writers, or setting up a program to bring performance artists into schools.

Thinking beyond traditional estate planning, what is the legacy you would like to leave?

During our discovery process with Gina, a wealthy widow in her seventies, we learned that she had a passion for music. Music had played a big role in her life, from her first piano lesson at eight, to her position as church organist for 30 years. Gina supported the Youth Symphony, an organization that sorely needed funds to continue providing opportunities for musically gifted children. She loved the idea of starting an endowment fund so that the Youth Symphony would have permanent funding. Gina knew that if she didn't do it herself, it would probably never happen, so she decided to leave the bulk of her estate to this new endowment fund.

But there was a problem: her two children were expecting a large inheritance. However, because of the clarity of her vision and the passion she felt for it, she was able to gather the strength necessary to tell her children.

"Your father and I paid for your college education so that you had no loans," she told them. "We gave you the down payments to get into your first homes. We lent you the money to start your businesses and we have given you the foundation for a successful life. Music is medicine for my soul, and I want other children to have the opportunities that I have had. I want your support for the legacy that I want to leave to the Youth Symphony Foundation. I don't love you any less for giving you a smaller inheritance." Not only did Gina create a wonderful legacy, but she also inspired her children to join her in the venture.

Gina's Blind Spot: Most people follow the tradition of leaving all their money to their children. Gina thought through this blind spot to discover a more meaningful legacy for her money.

One of the best illustrations of leaving a legacy that goes well beyond conventional planning can be found in the book *The Ultimate Gift*, by Jim Stovall. In 2005, Jim's book was made into a movie bearing the same title. We recommend reading the book or watching the movie to experience the power of defining your values and taking extraordinary steps to transfer all that is important to you to those you care about. *The Ultimate Gift* is very effective at illustrating the wonderful opportunities we all have to make a positive impact on the people and causes that are important to us.

Starting the Discovery Process

Open up your imagination, and take note of whatever comes to mind. Don't be afraid to consider all the possibilities, and don't discard even the slightest thoughts. You might want to begin with wishes. If you find yourself saying, "I wish I could spend more time with my grandkids," or "I wish I could speak Italian," or "I wish I could see the pyramids of Egypt," you just might have the beginnings of a vision.

To expand on a wish or a thought, ask yourself probing questions. What exactly are your wishes? Why do you want that? A wish to learn Italian may reveal your desire to live in Italy because you want to experience another culture. Your dream to see the pyramids might be based on a strong interest in ancient history and archeology. Without judgment, ask yourself questions and let each thought unfold.

As you begin the process, avoid asking yourself how your vision will become a reality. The means of obtaining it will be addressed later. Too often, people block their desires because they just don't see a way to get there from here. But if your vision is compelling, you can find a way to manifest it.

Man is so made that when anything fires his soul, impossibilities vanish.
JEAN DE LA FONTAINE, POET

Couples face an additional challenge because no two visions are exactly the same. Though you may share many interests with your partner, your vision and your destination are unique. To be successful, we recommend that you each explore your visions individually, then compare your findings and see how they can be combined.

Here are some questions to stimulate your thinking:

- If you had a very large financial windfall, what exciting things would you do? What would you buy? To whom would you give money? Why?
- What hobbies, passions, or projects did you put aside while building your career and family? Which ones would you like to resurrect? Why?
- What are your passionate causes or issues? What kind of impact would you like to make on them? Why?
- What have you never done that you'd love to do? Why?
- If you suddenly realized that today was the last day of your life, what would you regret and why?
- Twenty years from now, what memories and achievements would you like to be celebrating? With whom would you like to be celebrating them? Why?

Once you have identified a desire that excites you, step into that experience. Think about how you will feel when you have fulfilled your desire, and imagine the details: *I'm living in a small villa not far from Florence. I walk to a local café every morning for my coffee and order it in Italian.* Review your vision until it is absolutely clear in your mind. Write it down and keep it in a place where you will see it often. Let your vision evolve and grow, and remain alert to opportunities that arise related to it. Be aware that it could become strong enough to be your mission in life. Share this vision only with people who are like-minded and who will support you—this is *not* the time to involve naysayers.

Our client Heather had worked in corporate real estate consulting for many years. She was quite successful and made a very good income, but the travel, political pressures, and heavy workload were becoming wearisome. Because her entire career had been in this one field, she didn't see any options for herself.

Nearing burnout, Heather hurt her back and had to rest for several weeks. Unable to work, she decided to write a book to keep herself occupied. Heather had always enjoyed writing but rarely had time for anything but contracts and proposals. She decided to write a humorous novel, and when the book was done, she researched how to find an agent and get published.

"Fortunately," she says, "I was very naïve. If I'd known how 'impossible' it would be to get published, I probably never would have started. But because I didn't know any better, I headed forward, found an agent within a month, and sold my first book less than a week after that."

Heather has since left real estate and has made a career of freelance and creative writing. Although she makes less money, she loves the flexibility of her life and is much happier.

"I know that what I did is statistically impossible—but we aren't statistics, are we?"

Heather's Blind Spot: Heather felt it wasn't practical to quit a job that paid well or leave a successful career path to pursue an uncertain dream.

Discovering Your Blind Spots

Your assumptions are your windows on the world. Scrub them off every once in a while, or the light won't come in.

ALAN ALDA, ACTOR

As you uncover your vision, it's also important to uncover your blind spots regarding wealth and money. They may be obstructing your ability to create a better future.

Brian and Kate are a lively, intelligent couple in their early fifties. Brian is a mathematics professor at a local university and Kate recently became an attorney with a focus on corporate mergers and acquisitions. Though Kate's new career enhanced their financial situation tremendously, they found themselves fighting over money more than at any other time in their marriage.

Kate and Brian had married right out of college and immediately started a family. Brian earned his teaching credential and worked his way up through the academic ranks while Kate stayed at home with their two children. When the children reached their teens, Kate finally pursued her dream of attending law school. Within a few years of earning her degree, Kate became the major breadwinner of the family, earning more than twice Brian's salary. Their tension over finances grew.

"I'm proud of what Kate has done," Brian told us. "Yet somehow the money bothers me and I don't know why."

It took Brian a while to identify the blind spot at the source of the tension. He remembered his father working 80-hour weeks to support his family: a wife whose health was delicate, and four children, including an autistic brother. Brian's frail but always positive mother was very appreciative of her husband's efforts, complimenting him frequently and telling the children how proud they should be of their father. His father's response was always the same: "It's no big deal. It's a man's job to take care of his family."

Like many men, Brian tied much of his self-worth to his ability to provide for his family. When he identified this blind spot, Brian and Kate were able to talk it through. Brian acknowledged the special circumstances that had forced his father to work so hard, and Kate became more aware of showing her appreciation for all the ways Brian contributed to their family. Her earning power became a benefit, not a source of contention, so they could joyfully use both of their incomes to plan their future.

Brian's Blind Spot: Brian let ingrained attitudes stop him from communicating about money issues.

There is only one success…to be able to spend your life in your own way, and not to give others absurd maddening claims upon it.
CHRISTOPHER MORLEY, WRITER AND EDITOR

Still having a hard time discovering your personal vision? Blind spots often prevent people from even entertaining the notion of a broader view.

Nancy Kline's book, *Time to Think,* can be a helpful tool for ridding yourself of blind spots. In a section titled "Incisive Questions," she notes that strong, direct questions can remove assumptions that are stopping you from discovering your vision, and can free your mind to think with a fresh outlook:

If you want to take action, but are stuck, ask yourself, "What am I assuming here that is stopping me?" Listen to the answer, which might be, "I am assuming that I don't deserve success here." Then remove it: "If I knew that I do deserve success, what would I do right now?"

Many people need an outside observer, such as a friend or an advisor, to help them discover their blind spots. Look for someone who will help you discern for yourself what it is that you want. Have them ask you questions, listen for your answers, and ask more questions based on those answers to delve deeper into how you think and feel about a subject. This process will often allow you to expose your blind spots. Nancy Kline's book is a useful resource for helping you through this exercise.

Clear Yet Flexible

As your life progresses, so should your vision. You change, grow, and are exposed to new possibilities, and sometimes, life steps in and makes you change your priorities:

> Marilyn and Bob had worked hard to start building their dream home, an 8,000-square-foot house with a spacious outdoor entertainment area. Like all such projects, it had taken much more money and time than they had anticipated, and their home had been under construction for nearly three years. Though they wanted to travel and spend time with their grandchildren during this time, they felt they couldn't. Their business was financing this enormous project, and they didn't feel they could afford to take time off.
>
> One day, Marilyn was diagnosed with breast cancer. The treatment would slow her down substantially and force Bob to cut back on work to take care of her. The house was put on hold. Fortunately, at the end of her chemo and radiation treatment, Marilyn recovered her health.
>
> As you can imagine, the experience rearranged their priorities. They realized the unfinished house would only require more of their time and money, and it became less important than spending time with loved ones and experiencing adventures. They sold the house unfinished, and spent their resources pursuing what really mattered to them.
>
> **Marilyn and Bob's Blind Spot:** Marilyn and Bob didn't know what they truly wanted until they were faced with a life-changing event. Answering questions

like, "If you only had one year to live, how would you spend it?" will help clarify what is most important to you.

Asking yourself questions like, "If I only had a year to live, how would I spend it?" will help clarify what is most important to you.

Don't wait for a life-changing event to discover your vision. Most people need help to discover what's important to them now. Maybe you are lucky enough to have people in your life who can help you, such as a close friend, a relative, or a spiritual advisor. You can also hire people with this expertise, such as a counselor, a life coach, or a financial advisor who integrates this life-planning approach in their financial services.

Core Values

What good will it be for a man if he gains the whole world, yet forfeits his soul?
    MATTHEW 16:26

In recent decades, some companies have touted their core values as the reason for their business success. Southwest Airlines attributes its success to its belief in encouraging an entrepreneurial spirit in its employees, emphasizing personal responsibility, initiative, and the use of sound, independent judgment. While other retail stores have failed, Nordstrom has increased its sales because of its emphasis on superior customer service. Hassle-free returns are the norm at Nordstrom, and salespeople regularly write thank-you notes to their customers. For decades, Disney has been extremely successful in its mission of entertaining the world by exemplifying its core values of wholesomeness and imagination.

Most people don't spend very much time talking or thinking about their personal core values, which can be defined as key concepts and ideals that guide their lives and help them make important decisions. When people live by their unspoken core values, they feel good about themselves and in harmony with the world, but when they stray from these values, they tend to feel at odds, or, as one client put it, "uncomfortable in our own skin."

Core values are like blind spots, except they help you discover your vision rather than limit you. They are the specific qualities that you cherish, like compassion, integrity, tradition, or independence. They may be areas to which you want to devote your time and energy, such as education, personal growth, family, or helping others. They may be the very qualities that brought you your success, such as self-reliance, competence, creativity, and practicality. Others may share some of your values, but the combination of core values that make your life worthwhile is unique.

> Howard, a general contractor who ran a successful business building custom homes, believed strongly in the values that sports can teach: teamwork, fair play, preparation, and practice. He had been involved in his children's sports activities when they were young, coaching them and practicing with them. Once his children had grown up, his only sports involvement was as a spectator.
>
> As Howard dove into the discovery process, he realized that mentoring young people and teaching the lessons of sports were still very important to him.
>
> "Through my company and personally, I had always financially supported a myriad of local charities, but it never felt that great. I honestly didn't even know what some of them did. When I started focusing on the two things that were really important to me—kids and sports—I got really inspired." Now Howard not only supports four local Little League teams for at-risk children, he also developed a training program for coaches to make sure the underlying lessons of sports are taught as well. He has trained several of his employees, and, with their help, the program has spread throughout the region.
>
> **Howard's Blind Spot:** Howard wasn't fully aware of what he really cared about. When he discovered it, he was able to make that passion a focal point in his life.

What do core values have to do with wealth? Everything, especially if you are seeking the treasures of wealth. When your wealth supports your specific core values, your sense of satisfaction will be tremendous. Once you know the *what* and the *why* of your vision, it's time to tackle the *how*. Before you can decide how you will get where you want to be, you need to know where you are right now.

A goal without a plan is just a wish.
ANTOINE DE SAINT-EXUPERY, WRITER AND AVIATOR

TAKING ACTION: Clarifying Your Vision

1. Start a vision journal by writing down your answers to the questions on page 29.

2. For each wish that you uncover, write a statement that reflects your vision of that wish as if it were already in place, and explain the reason behind it. For example, "I have a beautiful home in the country because I enjoy having a place that is peaceful and quiet, where I can relax with special friends and family." As you do this, you will begin to create a vision that is truly unique to you. You will know that your vision is real and truly desirable when your passion for making it a reality takes over and you cannot wait to start moving forward. You may even create a vision that is intense enough that it becomes your mission or purpose in life.

3. Spend time adding detail to each vision. How will the vision look? How will it feel? Write down everything you can imagine about it, keeping all of your writing in the present tense. "My beautiful home in the country has fragrant fruit trees that bloom in the spring. It has several guest rooms, each one decorated simply and casually."

4. Once you have clarified and compiled your vision, discuss it with your partner or other people who are significant to your life journey. Discuss where your individual visions intersect and where they differ.

5. Think and write about your money blind spots. What are your beliefs about money? Do these beliefs still serve you well? Do you have strong emotional reactions to certain financial issues? Do these reactions still fit who you are today?

6. Using the exercises in Appendix A, define your core values. How are these values reflected in the way you use your resources? Are there new ways you can express these core values?

7. Using your visions and values as a basis, develop specific goals. Make sure that your goals are detailed and time bound. See Appendix A for further goal-setting tips.

8. If you have difficulty developing a vision for your life, find someone you trust to discuss your deepest feelings. This could be a friend, relative, mentor, or spiritual advisor, or you can hire someone such as a counselor, life coach, or financial planner who includes life planning as part of their practice.

CHAPTER FOUR

Step Two—Your Red Dot™

We can have facts without thinking but we cannot have thinking without facts.

JOHN DEWEY, PHILOSOPHER AND PSYCHOLOGIST

In the last chapter, you started defining wealth's treasures for yourself: the visions, dreams, and passions that you would like your wealth to support, and your ultimate destination. Your next step is to map out the best route to this destination. To do this, you need to be very clear on where you stand today. We call the process of determining your starting point the Red Dot.

You've seen the red dot in malls, hospitals, and airports. It sits on a huge map of a complicated facility, with the clear message, "You Are Here." It doesn't indicate, "You Are Approximately Here" or, "This Is Where You Were just a Short Time Ago." It points out exactly where you are at this moment in time. While a GPS generates your starting point via various satellites, you must generate your financial Red Dot yourself.

To map out the best route to your ultimate destination, you need to know exactly where you stand today.

There are two components to the Red Dot:

1. What you have: A very detailed net worth statement (including the Asset Microscope found in Appendix B), which we will discuss in the first half of this chapter.
2. What you need: An assessment of your current level of financial independence, and a calculation of the cost of your desired lifestyle. We will address this component in the second half of this chapter.

Many financial planners are happy to begin the planning process with a simple net worth statement, an estimate of how much you usually spend on an annual basis, and a calculator. This approach will only tell you, "You Are Approximately Here." To ensure that you attain the true treasures of your wealth, the Red Dot goes much deeper.

The Red Dot

- creates a detailed **net worth statement** that can easily be updated so you have a clear picture of where you are at any time;
- ensures that the **documentation** of each asset and liability is clear and accessible;
- organizes data in a way that **clarifies** your assets and liabilities;
- allows you to **simplify** your holdings and the documentation supporting them; and
- takes into account your **"soft" assets**, such as your health, talents, relationships, and community connections; and your **"soft" liabilities**, such as your blind spots, any bad money habits, or detrimental attitudes such as an aversion to numbers.

Creating the Red Dot version of a net worth statement takes considerable time and effort for most people. (See Appendix B for the Red Dot Net Worth Statement format and the Asset Microscope format.) If you have participated in financial planning before, you may think your affairs are in pretty good order, but by digging into the details required by this process, you might realize that an ex-spouse is still listed as beneficiary on an insurance policy, or that the family foundation never got the funding you intended. You might stumble onto a partnership structure that is long past its usefulness, or find that you never re-titled your assets to fund the living trust discussed years before.

Similarly, some people dread exposing their entire financial picture. They fear that it will be less than they hoped or will have some serious flaws, which in turn will reflect on their character or intelligence. Like visiting the dentist after a long hiatus, they can't imagine that the news will be good. In fact, as you likely know from other experiences in your life, overcoming a daunting obstacle is empowering. The reality of whatever you feared is rarely as bad as you anticipated, and once you know the score, it's easy to come up with an action plan to address any issues that have come to light.

You've probably already done much of the basic work required for an expanded net worth statement. The process of creating your Red Dot involves collecting all of that data and documentation, then making an inventory

Once you know where you stand, it's easy to come up with an action plan to tackle any issues that have come to light.

of it, organizing it, and simplifying it. If the system you have in place for organizing your personal finances already does this, you may not need to go through this process. To find out how your picture of your personal finances compares, answer the following questions:

- If you had to make a fast decision about selling a particular asset, would you be able to put your finger on its cost basis within minutes to weigh the tax consequences?
- If you suddenly became incapacitated, would your spouse or children be able to walk into your office and find all of the financial information needed to make critical decisions?
- If you were out of the country, could you easily tell someone the location of the documentation for a particular asset?
- If you and your spouse simultaneously died in an accident, would your heirs know where to find your critical documents, your most current wills, and your funeral wishes?
- If you were offered early retirement or a proposal to purchase your business, would you be able to take stock of your entire financial picture quickly to determine the right decision?
- If someone in one of your partnership structures dies, could you quickly research and understand the ramifications of the event?

If you could not confidently answer "yes" to all of these questions, don't feel bad. The people we know who have been the most successful in building wealth rarely attain this level of organization—usually because they're too busy. Organization takes time, and it doesn't seem important compared to other activities. However, by putting in the initial effort to create your Red Dot, or by paying someone else to do it for you, you can eliminate the inefficiency, unnecessary complexity, and stress that often results from being unorganized. Not only does the Red Dot help you map the route to your ultimate destination, it is also extremely useful for handling your current activities. The next time your accountant asks for an obscure bit of information and you locate it easily and quickly, or your broker calls for a quick decision on your portfolio, you'll experience the confidence and power that comes with having completed this process.

Red Dot™ for Couples

The process of creating your Red Dot is especially valuable for couples, since each person has only a piece of the picture, like our clients Peter and Sally.

> When Peter was just starting his business, he hesitated to let his wife, Sally, see the financial risks he was taking. He felt it would cause unnecessary stress in her already hectic life raising their four young children. Over the years, they maintained the code of "Don't ask, don't tell." Peter gave Sally a monthly allowance to run the household and managed their finances by himself. Under Peter's good stewardship, they were fortunate enough to drive nice cars, purchase a second home in Hawaii, and give money to charities.
>
> As the business grew and became extremely profitable, Sally grew resentful because she saw Peter writing larger and larger checks for fancier cars and extravagant business trips. She had no idea that their net worth had grown to over $20 million, and Peter had no idea that Sally was scrimping and stressing to make her household allowance cover each month's expenses. By going though the Red Dot process, they were both able to view their entire financial picture. Communication opened up between them, and they were able to make intelligent decisions together about how to spend their money. Stress and resentment disappeared because they each felt confident in their finances and empowered by their wealth.
>
> **Peter and Sally's Blind Spot:** Sally worried needlessly while Peter kept financial information to himself.

How the Red Dot™ Net Worth Differs

The Red Dot Net Worth Statement includes information not ordinarily seen on a net worth statement. It is designed to easily and quickly provide your personal representative with information about your assets in the event of your death or incapacitation. The Red Dot statements are clear, complete, and well organized and provide all the information you, your personal representative, or your heirs may need to move quickly and make intelligent decisions.

Beyond all the usual information found on a net worth statement, the Red Dot captures all in one place

- your account numbers;
- titling of assets such as joint tenancies, community property, and living trusts;
- details of all debt, including interest rate and term;
- beneficiaries of all retirement plans, life insurance policies, and annuities; and
- the cost basis of all assets subject to capital gains upon sale.

Your Red Dot should also note the location of all legal documents. During the Red Dot process, you will review each and every document to determine what documentation you have and whether it is accurate.

When all your assets and liabilities have been defined and valued, you should look at the complete picture and ask yourself some questions. What areas obviously need improvement? Is every investment performing well? If not, how can you improve performance? Can accounts be consolidated to simplify the financial structure and its management? Which assets do you want to keep for your heirs?

Next, apply the criteria of relevance. Does it still make sense to maintain certain legal structures, like a C-Corp, S-Corp, LLC, or family limited partnership? Are all of your cash accounts still necessary? Should existing debts remain in place or should they be restructured or paid off? During this part of the process, give all of your important advisors the total picture of your net worth so they can weigh in effectively on any issues that arise.

Mary and Joe had built a very successful real estate firm in collaboration with Mary's brother. Through the years, they became involved with several general and limited partnerships to purchase real estate. Joe liked to invest in various stock and bond investments as well. Their assets grew—not only in worth, but also in complexity.

After they sold their company, Mary and Joe wanted to be less involved in their many investments but didn't think it was possible. After completing the Red Dot process, they were thrilled to discover that they could not only simplify their holdings, but improve them as well:

- Four stock and bond accounts were reduced to two, and five non-performing stocks were sold.
- Six retirement accounts were consolidated into two and the investments were integrated into a portfolio and diversified through proper asset allocation.

- Two limited partnerships that had become cumbersome and stressful were sold.
- Another partner's interest in one investment was bought out so Mary and Joe could have full control.
- Two income-producing properties were identified and repositioned so they could be passed on to Mary and Joe's children.
- An insurance policy that increased estate tax liability was transferred out of the estate.
- A mortgage was paid off to enhance a property's income stream.
- Two assets intended to be part of a living trust were correctly re-titled.

Mary and Joe's Blind Spot: Past financial transactions that went unexamined created needless complexity for Mary and Joe.

Completing the net worth portion of the Red Dot takes some effort, but the clarity and peace of mind it offers are well worth it. Like the American forces entering the Battle of Midway, you will be confident that all future decisions and actions are based on detailed, accurate, and up-to-date information.

TAKING ACTION: Your Red Dot™

1. Determine whether you will put together all of the information needed for the Red Dot yourself, or if you'd prefer to hire someone else to do it. If you want someone else to do it, contact your CPA or financial planner to see if they can do this for you. If they cannot, ask them to refer you to someone who can.

2. Locate the pertinent documents needed to fill out the forms in Appendix B. Fill out the forms, noting any items that are missing.

3. Verify that each document has been fully executed and is current.

4. Make a list of action items needed to complete the net worth and Asset Microscope portions of the Red Dot, such as finding missing or non-executed documents and getting questions answered. Delegate these tasks or do them yourself until your Net Worth Statement and Asset Microscope are complete.

5. With your financial planner or other trusted advisor, review your current holdings. Could your accounts or assets be simplified? Are they still relevant? Are your investments performing to expectation? Turn these findings into action items that you or your advisors will complete.

6. Set up a schedule for updating and reviewing your Red Dot. You may want to update it annually unless there are reasons to do it more frequently.

Defining Financial Independence

Though I am grateful for the blessings of wealth, it hasn't changed who I am. My feet are still on the ground. I'm just wearing better shoes.

OPRAH WINFREY, TALK SHOW HOST

The second step of preparing the Red Dot is determining your financial independence status. Are you financially independent? If not, when will you be financially independent?

If you are like most people, those questions may leave you a bit overwhelmed. No matter your net worth, you probably don't think you are financially independent. You might believe that financial independence is in the realm of the ultra-wealthy, like Warren Buffett or Larry Ellison. Is there a magic number that defines financial independence? It certainly must be more than what you have, right?

Financial independence has several definitions. Some say that it is the point when you are able to cover your own financial needs and you no longer rely on your parents. Others say that it is when you no longer have to work to survive, when your income and assets cover all your basic needs. Yet others claim that you are financially independent when you can do and have whatever you want, whenever you want, whether you are working or not.

> Financial independence is as much about being confident as it is about having enough money.

In our experience, financial independence is as much about having a confident mindset as it as about having enough money. Many of the families with whom we work have plenty of money but, surprisingly, not nearly enough confidence. As a result, they are driven to keep accumulating, piling up assets in the hope that one day there will be "enough."

Are We There Yet?

In his book *Beyond Success*, Randall Ottinger interviewed numerous wealthy individuals on either side of the wealth divide—those who knew they were financially independent and those who didn't. He concluded that, "in order to cross the wealth divide permanently they must cross it psychologically by accepting the fact they have wealth beyond what is needed in their lifetime."

But how much is that? The truth is that financial independence—the number that says you have enough—is different for different people. A 75-year-old environmentalist who lives simply and alone, rides his bike everywhere, and is perfectly healthy will certainly need a different amount to last through his lifetime than the couple in their forties who have three homes, a daughter with disabilities, and parents with limited incomes.

Sometimes the concept of "enough" seems elusive. You may imagine that you must continue to expand your lifestyle, or that unknown disasters are waiting to befall you. You may be afraid that a bad turn in the economy could wipe you out. You may have plenty of assets but limited cash flow, or vice versa. Many of us are just never able to imagine that we've actually "arrived."

One of our biggest struggles as advisors is convincing those who have accumulated wealth that they are, in fact, financially independent and that they really do have enough to begin spending it and pursuing goals other than building their nest egg. In a study conducted by Boston College, only 36 percent of those with an excess of $5 million in assets felt financially secure.[1]

K nowing you have enough comes from understanding where you are and how far your assets will take you.

So how can you feel financially secure? Knowing you have enough doesn't come from an in-depth understanding of the stock market or from years of studying tax laws and inflation trends. Knowing you have enough comes from understanding where you are—your Red Dot—and seeing how far your assets will take you.

The question that haunts most people in the United States, even people who have millions, is "Will I have enough?" Will you have enough money to do all the things that you want and to cover all the unexpected things that might happen until the day you die, whenever that might be? The answer may seem unattainable, but there is a process for dealing with this question. The process comprises the following steps:

1. Gather information on all your assets that you'll use in retirement (which you did during the net worth portion of the Red Dot process).
2. Make meaningful assumptions about variables, such as rates of return, inflation, and unexpected expenses. (Your advisors can help you with this if you're unsure.)

3. Develop your Lifestyle Price Tag, including travel funds, hobby expenses, and extraordinary costs. (This is addressed later in this chapter.)
4. Run projections with different scenarios and contingencies.

Appendix D addresses the information you will need for a projection. It also includes a discussion of variables that are important to understand and describes the nuances of a good projection that will give you the confidence you seek. For most people, using an advisor such as a CERTIFIED FINANCIAL PLANNER™ practitioner or a financial planning–accredited CPA to run a projection is the fastest, most comprehensive way to get answers. Acquainting yourself with the parameters in Appendix E will put you in the best position to provide good information that will get you the answers you need.

The Ah-Ha Moment

Over the years, we've often had the pleasure of witnessing that magical moment when people who have worked hard to save and preserve their wealth, but have worried about finances, finally realize they truly do have enough.

When Helen and Doug first came to us, they found it difficult to discuss money even with each other. Helen refused to attend the first planning meetings because she thought we were going to put her on an even stricter budget than the severe budget her husband had her following. After listing all of their real estate and retirement assets and running a financial projection using their Lifestyle Price Tag (as described later in this chapter), we advised them that they could sell or close down their business and still have much more money than they would ever use in their lifetimes.

Like most people who have amassed fortunes, they needed us to run and rerun many varied scenarios for the truth to sink in: they had enough. In fact, they had much more than enough. One of their biggest hurdles to realizing that fact was the diversity of their assets. They had assumed that this diversity created security, but in reality, it created uncertainty about where they were financially at any given time. With a little help consolidating retirement accounts into one reporting system and assistance in hiring a CPA to keep track of their real estate holdings, Helen and Doug felt secure enough to begin to wind down and simplify their business activities. Two years after they first came to us for planning, they closed down their business.

This, of course, created a new issue: "How will we now spend our money?" At the date of this writing, they haven't quite figured it out, but a holiday card we received from Helen proved that their perception of their wealth had changed. It said, "Happy holidays, and thanks for letting me live budget-free!"

Helen and Doug's Blind Spots: Helen thought that if she faced the reality of her financial situation, she would have to change her behavior. Also, a complex financial situation prevented Helen and Doug from seeing the big picture.

Not all entrepreneurs close down their businesses when they recognize that they have enough. Sometimes, the confidence that they have enough actually allows them to build a bigger dream.

Kim and Stewart spent three decades growing their second-generation family business beyond what they had ever imagined. Since they both worked in the business, it was easy for them to get consumed by its details and drudgery, as well as by the instinctive drive to keep it growing. The concept of retirement wasn't something Kim and Stewart ever discussed. They gave to local charities, typically between $1,000 and $2,000 at a time, but were not involved in the activities of those charities. They wanted to take vacations and be with their grandchildren more. Though they didn't really talk about it, both of them were terrified of retirement. As long as they focused on growing the business, they felt confident their financial security would be protected.

When Kim and Stewart came to see us, we broached the subject of financial independence. After 30 hard years in the construction business, the concept of such freedom was scary but enticing. After completing the Red Dot process and understanding their own Lifestyle Price Tag, they saw that they had amassed a net worth of $8 million. Based on their lifestyle, vision, and desires, Kim and Stewart realized that the most they would ever use of this amount was $5.2 million.

Kim started thinking about building houses for the people who were struggling in the tough neighborhood where she grew up. Stewart had always dreamed of building a health clinic in a remote village in Mexico. Their $2.8 million surplus was more than enough to do both. The realization was exhilarating! They decided to keep growing the business for now, but their new perspective affected their attitude toward money and time. Stewart started taking every Friday off to play golf, and Kim volunteered to watch her grandsons one day a week so that her daughter could have a little downtime. They no longer feared the peaks and valleys that life might bring because they were 100 percent confident that they had enough.

> **Kim and Stewart's Blind Spot:** Kim and Stewart didn't think that they would be able to help others in a really meaningful way until they knew they had enough for themselves, but they were so afraid of not having enough that they refused to look at their situation.

Discovering Your Lifestyle Price Tag™

How much will be enough for you? Traditional retirement planning conversations go something like this: The advisor asks you how much you spend each year. You throw out a number. Your advisor usually assumes that 80 percent of this number will be sufficient for retirement. He or she runs some modeling magic and gives you retirement projections based on that quick annual spending figure you offered. Voilà! You've got a retirement plan.

In fact, this traditional approach ignores the fact that the core of the planning is based on that vague number you threw out. The anxiety and nervousness people often bring to a retirement planning session—where they will finally find out whether what they've got will stack up against what they'll need to last through their lives—has them leaping to the projection stage. Traditional planning results in financial projections that may look good on paper but are in fact vague and superficial. The figure of how much you spend each year—your detailed Lifestyle Price Tag—is critical to discovering wealth's treasure of confidence. Being accurate with your Lifestyle Price Tag often means the difference between a retirement plan that allows you to get by and a financial independence number that lets you live the life you've always envisioned for yourself. It is also the difference between a retirement plan that leaves you feeling vaguely uneasy and a plan that gives you the sense of *enough*, that gives you confidence and direction. It is not a retirement plan that confines you to a fixed income, but a financial independence plan that supports possibilities.

An accurate Lifestyle Price Tag is often the difference between just getting by and financial independence.

What is a Lifestyle Price Tag? First of all, it's not a budget. A budget looks primarily at the income you have, then makes decisions on how you can spend based on that income. In other words, your income determines your lifestyle. People resist listing their expenses as a budget because the word "budget" conjures up the sense of being restricted. We prefer the term "Lifestyle Price Tag" because it reflects the concept of having plenty of resources to support an enjoyable life. A budget is like squeezing into a pair of tight pants; a Lifestyle Price Tag is more like wearing a comfortable shirt.

Many of our clients want to see three Lifestyle Price Tag scenarios:

1. Bare bones—Using basic yearly expenses with no frills, perhaps using a reverse mortgage toward the end of their life
2. Comfortable—Adding the extras to bare bones
3. Bountiful—Including every wish they can imagine: yearly trips overseas, visiting children and grandkids frequently, taking the entire family to Hawaii regularly, extra money allocated for unknown or specialty medical expenses, regular generous gifts to favorite charities, etc.

When calculating a Lifestyle Price Tag, start by looking at your *life*. What is important to you? How do you want to live? How much money do you want to contribute to others? What trips do you wish to take? What rainy days do you want to save for? Take all of that into consideration when you are working on your Lifestyle Price Tag.

Life Stages

Obviously, your Lifestyle Price Tag will be different at various stages of your life. When you were first starting out, you might have been on a pretty tight budget that allowed you to pay the rent and put gas in the car. Through the years, your income expanded to allow you to buy a home, pay for your children's education, save for the future, and enjoy some discretionary income. Each stage of your life had a certain Lifestyle Price Tag: the amount of money you spent to live the life you chose for yourself.

Later life has different life stages, too, and different Lifestyle Price Tags. The Go-Go Years (typically between 60 and 75) are the years in which you begin to work less or cease working altogether. You may be quite active, perhaps traveling the world, taking up new hobbies or interests, and visiting family and grandchildren more often. During the Slow-Go Years (typically between 75 and 85), you might reduce your activities a bit. Often you will need to address health challenges during this period. The No-Go Years (typically over the age of 85) are those in which you slow down substantially, and perhaps move into a retirement community. Each of these stages has its own Lifestyle Price Tag, shifting from the higher expenditures of the Go-Go Years to the lesser and more stable expenses of the No-Go Years.

It's All About You

Your Lifestyle Price Tag is just as unique as your ultimate destination. It doesn't matter what your neighbors or the average American consumer spends; they don't have your unique dreams and desires, your specific assets, or your particular core values. Their treasures are not yours. John and Janet realized this when they calculated their Lifestyle Price Tag.

> As a couple, John and Janet had amassed $5 million in net worth the old-fashioned way: they spent less than they made. Without really being aware of how much they had saved or spent, they maintained a strong pattern of living frugally. By their mid-fifties, John and Janet found themselves wishing they could afford to do some of the things their friends were doing: buy a boat or fancier home, travel first class, or join a country club. They were frustrated but didn't know if they could afford to do those things without destroying all they had worked to build.
>
> Through the Red Dot and Lifestyle Price Tag calculations, they realized that they could afford to do all the things that their neighbors were doing—but they also discovered that they didn't really want to. They realized that although travel was a priority of theirs, they'd rather spend their money designing their own trips than buying package tours. They decided against a vacation home but opted for an international time-share that gave them more flexibility. They decided against the country club membership in favor of giving more to their favorite church and to charities. The discovery process taught them how to assess their true financial position and to explore their genuine, unique desires, and the power of clarity they achieved through these exercises allowed them to make decisions that improved their lives.
>
> **John and Janet's Blind Spot:** John and Janet got caught in the comparison trap, thinking they should buy the luxuries their friends had.

So how do you begin to determine your Lifestyle Price Tag? Appendix C has a worksheet that lists all the information you will need. First, track your current spending by examining your checkbook, ATM withdrawals, and credit card statements. Be aware of any proceeds that you may have spent from the sale of assets. Alternatively, rather than tracking your past spending, you can track your expenditures over the next several months. Keep in mind that one or two months are often not reflective of an entire year. Be sure to include any additional spending that might occur during the holidays or for unexpected house maintenance.

Second, estimate large and infrequent expenses. Often, people want to set up a "fun fund" so they have extra money for travel and other expenses during their Go-Go years. You might estimate $30,000 per year for your fun fund between the ages of 65 and 75, then only $15,000 per year from between the ages of 75 and 85. Buying cars during retirement is another large, infrequent expense. Some people might allocate $50,000 for a car every seven years, for example.

Next, imagine your money is in an imaginary account that will disappear if you don't use it. What things have you always wanted to do but haven't yet done? Take family vacations? Live abroad? Fund a charity? Estimate a price for each of those desires.

Finally, think of contingency plans. How would you handle healthcare issues that might arise? How could you help your children or parents in times of need? What if your current employment ceases? Write down all of your vague worries and estimate a cost for each one.

Once you have an entire picture based on your desires, concerns, visions, and the stage of your life, total up the entire cost. If it doesn't seem like enough, add 20 percent to it, just to be sure. This figure is the amount of income that you want to produce to ensure that the life you choose to live is fully funded—your Lifestyle Price Tag. **The amount of assets required to produce this income is your financial independence number.**

Many clients find that becoming very clear and conscious of their Lifestyle Price Tag adds tremendously to their sense of confidence about their wealth. However, just as many people resist taking the process seriously.

John and Sue, both healthy and in their mid-sixties, asked us to run two financial independence projections for them. They did not want to spend the time calculating their Lifestyle Price Tag, so they roughly estimated that they would spend between $150,000 and $175,000 annually, two totally unsubstantiated numbers. Our first projection showed that John and Sue's assets would comfortably cover 25 more years at the $150,000 yearly spending level. However, if they wanted to spend $175,000 annually, they could only produce 18 years' worth of income. Since they both had parents who had lived well into their nineties, John and Sue became very motivated to determine exactly what level of income they really needed after seeing the difference it could make in their financial security.

John and Sue's Blind Spot: John and Sue did not realize that a rough estimate of their Lifestyle Price Tag wasn't enough. They didn't have the concrete evidence they needed to give them the confidence that they were financially secure.

Your Financial Independence Number

To calculate your financial independence number, you began with your vision, values, and goals (from Appendix A) and your Red Dot (from Appendix B), and related those to the Lifestyle Price Tag you calculated (Appendix C). Next, add in some meaningful assumptions to create projections. These assumptions are based on historical data and the experience of professionals, and they attempt to answer those unanswerable questions: How long will I live? Exactly how much will I need for health care? What will my money earn for the next 40 years? We've provided guidelines for determining these assumptions in Appendix D. Using educated assumptions, financial projections can measure your level of financial independence. If projections show that you aren't where you'd like to be, you can draw up a plan to achieve this goal by a certain date. Knowing you are financially independent, or even having a good idea of when you will be, can give you the confidence that will allow you to experience life in a different way. Money becomes a tool that empowers you to pursue whatever goals you set for yourself.

Even having a good idea of when you will be financially independent can give you the confidence to pursue your vision.

The graphs below illustrate the progression of assets under different scenarios and its relation to a client's financial independence status through his or her lifetime. These figures do not include a residence as an asset that could be liquidated to provide income to support financial independence. We assume you stay in your home until your death, but a reverse mortgage is a possibility within any scenario.

Graph One shows assets that deplete earlier than life expectancy. The client would need to decrease spending, work longer, or achieve a higher return on investment to maintain his financial independence.

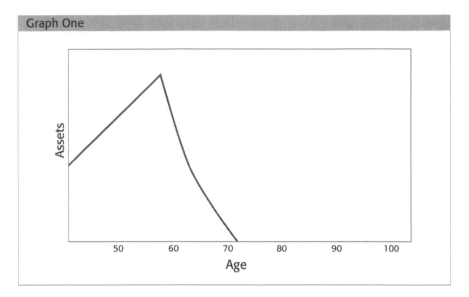

Graph Two depicts assets that will preserve enough money to cover the client's needs and desires even if she lives to be 100.

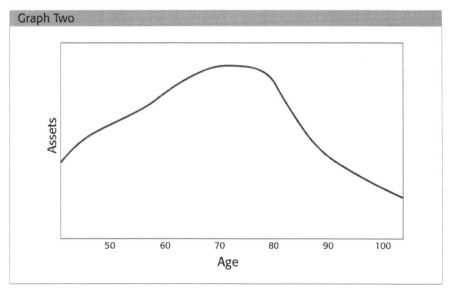

Graph Three illustrates assets that will continue to grow beyond the client's needs. With this scenario, the client can expand his vision of what is possible for his life. If he doesn't care to expand his current lifestyle, he can experience the joy of giving to friends and family or donating generously to favorite causes, and still be assured that all his needs will be met.

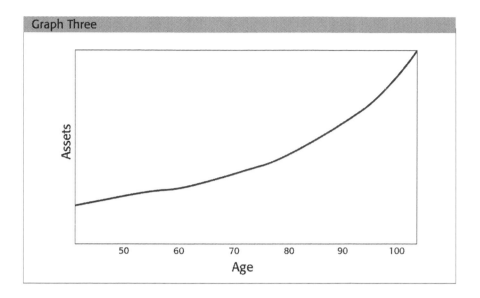

The Intangible Asset

Knowing that you are financially independent is a great feeling. It allows you to expand your dreams and release your creativity. It dissolves many of your worries and allows you to put your mental and emotional power to more productive use. If you are not quite financially independent based on your unique criteria, you've now determined the number that *will* be enough.

Gaining financial independence is an incredible milestone in life. You may find it hard to believe that you could ever have enough money to declare yourself financially independent, but if you are clear about your goals and visions, you have also discovered what is most important about your wealth. You can now focus your resources on those treasures, on what will make *you* happy, not what makes your friends and neighbors happy. With that clarity, you can assess your financial independence status today as it relates to your unique vision.

> *It is only after a person accepts that they have enough money and that wealth accumulation is no longer a singular goal that one is fully free to consider opportunities for...fulfillment.*
> RANDALL OTTINGER, AUTHOR AND PHILANTHROPIST

TAKING ACTION: Your Lifestyle Price Tag™ and Financial Independence

1. Using the form in Appendix C, calculate your Lifestyle Price Tag. When you have a total figure, see how you feel. If that number does not give you complete confidence, ask yourself why you feel uneasy. Perhaps you should add 20 to 40 percent to that figure, just to make yourself feel comfortable. Perhaps you should quantify your fears by putting price tags on them; for instance, estimating what your medical costs may amount to.

2. Using the information in Appendix D, calculate your own financial independence projection. If you have your advisor calculate it for you, bring the information you used in Appendices B and C to assist him or her with the projection.

CHAPTER FIVE

Step Three—Your Unique Strategy Filter™

Whatever course you decide upon, there is always someone to tell you that you are wrong. There are always difficulties arising which tempt you to believe that your critics are right. To map out a course of action and follow it to an end requires courage.

RALPH WALDO EMERSON, PHILOSOPHER

You've defined and clarified your personal vision, the life you choose to live today, the exciting dreams and goals for your future, and the legacies you intend to leave. You've inventoried your current assets and debts, assessed your level of financial independence, and determined your current and projected Lifestyle Price Tags. Now it's time to recognize the gap between where you are and where you want to be, and to create your Strategy Filter.

In this context, strategies are the means by which you achieve all the goals that will support your vision. Because your vision is unique, your means will be unique as well. Your financial advisors have been using filters all along to weigh the value of a variety of structures and investments for you. They consider the myriad aspects of each opportunity before they recommend anything to you. The problem is that the filters they have been using are based on their discipline and biases, the experiences of their other clients, a vague sense of your vision, and an incomplete picture of your total financial situation.

Now, however, because of the quality and depth of the work you did to discover and clarify your goals and core values, you can create a Strategy Filter that is unique to you and reflects the treasures you seek from your wealth.

A Look into the Gap

Reality is merely an illusion, albeit a very persistent one.
ALBERT EINSTEIN, THEORETICAL PHYSICIST

First, you will look at your gaps. Gaps are not inherently negative; they are simply the distance between where you are and where you want to be. For example, if you are at home and want to go to a certain restaurant, it's usually no big deal to get in your car, flip on your GPS, and, following the instructions, drive to your destination. If you're afraid they may run out of your favorite dish before you arrive, you might feel a bit more nervous about the distance between you and that restaurant. However, if you're running late for a dinner that is particularly important to your spouse, you don't have the restaurant address, your GPS is malfunctioning, and you know your spouse will be furious…well, now you've got a *negative* gap between where you are and where you want to be.

Similarly, some gaps between your current financial status and your desires will feel negative. Gaps that might undermine your sense of well-being today include burdens such as high credit card debt, fears that you will end up a bag lady, or a stockbroker you distrust (but who happens to be your favorite cousin's spouse). Negative gaps may also create anxiety about the future—your concerns about long-term care in case of disability, or fears for your children's financial well-being or careers. You may have finally realized that your cash flow doesn't actually support your current Lifestyle Price Tag,

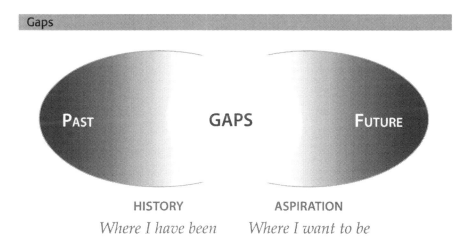

Gaps

PAST   GAPS   FUTURE

HISTORY   ASPIRATION
Where I have been   *Where I want to be*

and that you are eroding your asset base. You may have a volatile business partnership that could prove to be financially disastrous in the future, or your stock and real estate investments may have declined significantly.

These are the types of gaps that keep you up at night—especially before you confront them. In his book *Say Hello to the Elephants,* Tony Rose says that people often see obstacles and think, "Wow! That's an elephant! I better turn back," but even big gaps can be resolved when you face them squarely.

Other gaps are not negative, like the gaps between being acceptable versus being exceptional. Retiring from your career at 63 may feel *okay*, but leaving that career at 52 to pursue a new exciting venture would feel *great*. Leaving a few thousand dollars to your pet non-profit may feel *okay*, but endowing a new building for that same organization would feel *fantastic*. Paying off your home may feel *okay*, but creating a family compound in the Cayman Islands would feel *incredible*.

Vision gaps inspire you to wake up in the morning with a sense of excitement and purpose.

Whatever those exciting dreams, large or small, if they are beyond today's reality, they create a gap, and those are the gaps that inspire you to wake up in the morning with a sense of excitement and purpose.

You can deal with both types of gaps in the same way:

1. Specify what the gap is.
2. Create a strategy to close the gap.
3. Implement the strategy.

You probably won't be able to tackle all of your gaps at once, so you'll need to prioritize them. Deal with your biggest fears first—dreams and visions have little meaning if you feel that your very security is threatened, so whatever it is that keeps you awake at night with anxiety should be at the top of your list. List your gaps from Absolute Worst to Not So Bad. In other words, your very first priority is to fix the issue that causes you the most distress, whether it's your financial independence status, your incompetent tax preparer, or your credit card debt.

Remember that your prioritization of your gaps will be unique. Your accountant may be horrified by the level of your debt or the meager amount in your 401(k), but you may be more anxious about your lack of a long-term care plan. You're in the driver's seat, so you determine the priority.

Once you've inventoried the elephants in the room, list your vision gaps—the gaps between *okay* and *great*—in order of importance to you, not in order of ease to accomplish. This may fly in the face of conventional wisdom. Why not knock off the easiest gaps first? Because it's the excitement of your dreams that will pull you forward, energize you, and inspire your creativity. By focusing on the visions that most invigorate you, you'll find you accomplish your other goals naturally in the powerful wake you create.

Products and Strategies

Usually, the best plan incorporates many things: tax and estate planning strategies, investments or insurance products, and the reorganization of what is currently owned.

> Vince and Diana had operated a successful restaurant for many years and had accumulated a substantial portfolio of commercial real estate, mainly medical office buildings. Their three children were grown and were beginning to establish families of their own. Though they had loved the restaurant business, Vince and Diana wanted to slow down their pace of life and spend more time with their young grandchildren. They were fairly certain that they could sell the restaurant for a good price, but they couldn't figure out how to replace the income it had generated for them. Their real estate produced income, but they were tired of managing the properties. Additionally, Vince and Diana were uncertain about their estate plan, about what taxes would be due and how much would actually go to their heirs and charitable beneficiaries.
>
> To close the first gap—uncertainty about income after the sale of the restaurant—we created hypothetical projections for two separate investment strategies that could generate the $150,000 annual income they wanted to replace. These options incorporated existing assets and new possibilities. To close the second gap—the burden of managing their real estate—we researched two approaches: tenants in common (TIC) limited partner options, and Triple Net Lease structures, which provided income with less maintenance responsibility. Both offered the potential of a deferred exchange. Finally, to resolve the third gap—uncertainty about the disposition of their estate—we, along with their attorney, helped Vince and Diana review their current estate documents, converting the existing plan into specific distribution numbers (dollar amounts to each heir and charity) based on current asset values. We then helped them compare it to their ideal distribution plan to see what changes should be made.

Vince and Diana's Blind Spot: Vince and Diana couldn't move forward unless they saw specific strategies that would get them to their desired future.

Some gaps can be filled without any financial restructuring, but with careful listening and a little creative thinking.

Dave and Marti had both recently retired from successful careers. They had saved carefully and had positioned themselves well to begin the next chapter of their lives. They came to us before their annual visit to help settle a dispute over whether they should purchase a second home, a home that Dave really wanted but Marti adamantly opposed. We listened and probed, asking Dave what exactly he wanted from a second home.

"I like going to a place that is familiar, where I can just relax and put my feet up. Even on vacation, it's fun for me to putter around and fix things up around a house." As the conversation progressed, Marti mentioned that their close friends owned a second home in the foothills that they seldom used.

"They're always asking us to stay in the house whenever we want because they feel guilty that it just sits there most of the time," she said. "If we got a second home, it wouldn't be used much either."

We asked Dave if their friends' house was the kind of place he would enjoy. He said it was. Then we put forward the idea that Dave and Marti take their friends up on the invitation to spend time in the foothills home. Would that satisfy Dave's desire for a second home?

"It would be perfect! There's plenty to do up there and I know our friends would love having someone look after the place."

Dave and Marti's Blind Spot: A disagreement was preventing Dave and Marti from exploring creative solutions.

Dreams and gaps aren't always filled the way you expect they'll be—openness and creativity can offer numerous options.

The Place of Greatest Potential

In the absence of clearly defined goals, we become strangely loyal to performing daily trivia until ultimately we become enslaved by it.

ATTRIBUTED TO ROBERT HEINLEIN, SCIENCE FICTION WRITER

W here you want to be, where you are today, and the gaps between the two form your Strategy Filter.

When you are focused on the treasures of wealth, discovering your gaps brings you to the place of greatest potential. You've accumulated valuable information from your work so far: the discovery of where you want to be in the future, the reality of where you are today, and the gaps that keep the two apart. This information forms your personalized Strategy Filter. Only a few strategies will fit your particular situation.

For example, let's imagine someone who is not financially independent and will run out of money prior to his death (see Graph One on page 52). Closing that gap would likely be his highest priority. His Strategy Filter might include action items such as

- asset optimization—evaluating each of his assets to determine how to optimize their returns;
- a Lifestyle Price Tag review—reviewing, refining, and revising his Lifestyle Price Tag to determine what, if anything, he could give up or reduce; or
- income expansion options—working longer, developing a strategy to increase his earnings until retirement, working part-time during retirement, or developing a home-based business to increase his income during retirement, for instance.

Someone else might have a different scenario, perhaps one where her wealth will continue to grow as she ages (see Graph Three on page 53). This person is already financially independent, so her Strategy Filter dictates an entirely different approach. Her filter might include

- finding new opportunities for spending, not just on necessities;
- investing with less risk, since investments aren't needed for growth; or
- creating estate planning strategies that include giving money to children, grandchildren, and charities now.

Clearly, these two approaches are entirely different. These strategies may seem obvious, but many people haven't taken the time to find out whether they will run out of money before they die or if they are already financially independent, so they make decisions and apply strategies without any justification. Why should financially independent people say they can't afford to take trips when their investments go down temporarily? Why should they take too much risk in their portfolios when their wealth would continue to grow under a conservative approach? Conversely, why should people who aren't financially independent be overly generous with their children? Why should they invest very conservatively and forego growth?

As we've seen time and time again with our clients, once you have a complete picture of your finances and a clear sense of your vision, you will see which strategies are right for you. You've developed a personalized Strategy Filter, which is the accumulation of all of the work you've done to this point: discovering your mission, vision, values, and goals; completing your Red Dot to show your net worth and financial independence status; and finding and prioritizing your gaps. Using your unique Strategy Filter, all of your advisors can apply their best thinking and most creative ideas to the job of closing your gaps and getting you where you really want to be.

Without a good Strategy Filter, even the most capable and well-intentioned advisors cannot find appropriate solutions for you. They are missing the most important piece of the puzzle—who you are, what you want, and why. Our client Steve shared a story that illustrates this point.

> Years ago, Steve had a number of competent and enthusiastic advisors. One day, Steve's investment broker called him to let him know about an intriguing opportunity. After hearing his advisor out, Steve felt excited about the opportunity's potential. He called his CPA of 14 years to get another opinion. The CPA thought the idea might have merit, but had an opportunity of his own he wanted Steve to consider. Steve's call to his attorney elicited yet another investment possibility. Over the next week, Steve felt like a ping-pong ball, bouncing from call to call, idea to idea. He had lots of expertise at his fingertips, but no clarity.
>
> After doing some work to focus on the treasures he wanted from his wealth, Steve was able to create a clear and specific Strategy Filter. Now, when an opportunity presents itself, Steve simply looks at his priorities: increasing cash flow to invest back into his business, remaining debt-free except for his home, giving substantial tithes to his church, minimizing stress in his life, and having time and resources to travel abroad. If the opportunity doesn't address those priorities, Steve is able to let it pass and sleep well at night.

Steve's Blind Spot: Any opportunity seemed like a good idea when Steve failed to use a filter that focused on his priorities.

Your Strategy Filter not only informs your advisors, but also gives you a clear way to assess your current portfolio and screen new opportunities. At one time or other, most people get caught up in the financial strategy *du jour*, or that clever tax-avoiding structure in *Money Magazine*, or a tennis partner's latest high-yield venture. Some people may look at their existing holdings and wonder what function they serve in the overall scheme of things. With your unique Strategy Filter in place, there is no mystery. You know precisely what structures and investments serve your vision and how they do so.

I n order for your Strategy Filter to remain effective, it must evolve as your life does.

Keeping Current

As life changes, so does your vision for yourself. For your Strategy Filter to remain effective, it must evolve as your life changes. Our client Elizabeth discovered this recently.

Elizabeth and her husband, John, had built their wealth through real estate. John had an excellent eye for properties with potential and a good sense of the market. He enjoyed handling the day-to-day management of their holdings and built a good rapport with tenants, vendors, and brokers in the community.

After John's death, Elizabeth felt overwhelmed by their real estate investments. The responsibility of property ownership caused her a great deal of stress, and she felt trapped by it. Initially, Elizabeth was reluctant to make any changes. The properties had been chosen well and were still generating cash and appreciating. Friends told her she would be foolish to undo what John had built, and Elizabeth frankly didn't see any other options.

Elizabeth updated her vision, values, and goals and created a Strategy Filter that reflected her present reality and desires rather than the life she and John had shared in the past. In doing this, she realized that real estate was no longer a good fit. She now wanted the flexibility to travel and spend time with her children and grandchildren. She wanted more of her assets to be liquid, and she wanted an income stream that was passive, not requiring her active involvement. We discussed other investments that were more suited to her.

Having gained confidence through this clarity, Elizabeth prioritized her gaps and began selling the properties she liked least. She reinvested the money into long- and short-term bonds with a variety of maturation dates. Elizabeth contracted a property management firm to handle the remaining properties, and though the cost of this service cut into her cash flow, it gave her the freedom and peace of mind she desperately wanted. Later that year, an unsolicited offer came in to purchase another one of her buildings. Though she hadn't intended to sell more property just yet, her decision to accept the offer was easy and stress free. Elizabeth already had a good sense of the property's value and its cost basis through the Red Dot process. Although there was very little economic difference between selling this property and keeping it, Elizabeth was very clear that the decision to sell met her goals of simplicity and flexibility.

Elizabeth's Blind Spot: Elizabeth thought that assets inherited through the death of a spouse or family member should be kept and never sold.

Elizabeth created her unique Strategy Filter after her husband passed away, but we also encourage couples to explore their differences while both are still alive. As Ruth and Keith discovered, this contributes even more to peace of mind.

Ruth and Keith were in their seventies when they came to us to review their financial situation. Their goal was to have an investment portfolio and asset management system that would be appropriate for either of them, no matter who passed away first. Keith enjoyed investing in individual stocks and bonds in consultation with two different brokers he trusted. Ruth, however, was not astute in investment matters, and they both worried about how she might handle the complicated portfolio Keith had created if he died first. Ruth felt overwhelmed; she wanted a portfolio that was easy to understand and had a simple management system.

Based on their concerns, the strategy filter produced options ranging from

- keeping the portfolio as is, and trusting that Keith's faithful brokers would take good care of Ruth;
- hiring a professional money manager to oversee the portfolio;
- consolidating with one broker and putting everything in mutual funds;
- transferring all investments into bank certificates of deposit, which Ruth understood and felt comfortable with; or
- waiting until Keith died to decide.

> After considering and discussing each option, it was decided that they both liked the third option best. The broker who was chosen devised a hypothetical portfolio to show them how Ruth would get the income she needed if Keith predeceased her. Confidence in Ruth's financial future replaced their prior worry and insecurity.
>
> **Ruth and Keith's Blind Spot:** Like many couples, Ruth and Keith didn't know how to deal with the fact that the financially uninvolved spouse would have difficulties after the involved spouse died.

The clients we've talked about are no more investment savvy than most people. What makes them excellent investors and wealth strategists is the clear vision they have of their values and dreams, their current situation, and their priorities. They are focused on the treasures of wealth and are confident in the moves they make.

It's Not a Mystery

Strategy Filters are not esoteric, incomprehensible formulas created by some multi-degreed mathematical genius. As you've seen, they are simply the application of your core values and cherished dreams to your financial decisions. Some people's Strategy Filters are as straightforward as, "I want $100,000 per year in income, with no risk or involvement on my part, so I can pursue my creative career." Others have more complex Strategy Filters, like, "I want to build enough in assets to endow a fund of at least $4 million for homeless children, receive an annual net income for myself of $150,000, have a home fully paid for with no other debt, and have all of my investments in ecologically conscious funds." Your Strategy Filter is based on your vision, however simple or complex. Here are some examples of how they may apply to different people.

A Grandmother Raising Her Two Young, Recently Orphaned Grandchildren

She wants to pay off her debts and create an income stream so that she can retire and raise the children. She also wants to ensure that her grandchildren have college funds. Her filter would consider a 529 college savings plan with tax-free growth attractive because it could fund the children's education. She would not find illiquid investments attractive unless they paid good dividends, and she would lean toward low-risk investments. As she begins her new lifestyle raising her grandchildren, she would value liquidity and financial flexibility above all.

A 70-Year-Old Retired Bachelor with No Family

He wants to create an endowment for a museum of ethnic art. He's concerned about medical expenses as he ages, and wants to live independently for as long as possible. He wants to take one or two golf trips per year, but, other than that, is happy to live very simply and frugally. His filter might exclude making any investments that are high risk, but it would support buying long-term care insurance that has provisions for home healthcare, allowing him to bring help to his home. He might want to add some high-income investments to increase his cash flow to fund his golf trips, and he'll want to redraft his will so that all of his estate goes to the museum he loves.

A Couple in Their Sixties with Two Adult Children

This couple wants to leave a good portion of their assets to their children. Although their son is financially astute and responsible, their daughter has had intermittent problems with drug abuse. They don't want their son to be responsible for his sister when they die, yet they want to provide some form of security for her. Because of this filter, they shouldn't create an estate plan that simply divides the assets equally and distributes them outright to each child. They should consider two options for their daughter: either setting up an annuity to provide income for her over her lifetime, or putting her inheritance into a trust with a designated third-party trustee. The trust could provide her with income and access to principal for specific expenditures.

Your Strategy Filter is based on the in-depth, honest work you do during the discovery process. It provides direction for all of your advisors' recommendations and all the financial decisions you make, allowing you to move smoothly into your Fulfillment Plan.

TAKING ACTION: Your Gaps and Your Strategy Filter™

1. Inventory the gaps between where you are and where you would like to be. Write them all down—large and small, negative and positive.
2. Prioritize your gaps. Prioritize negative gaps from Absolute Worst to Not So Bad. Prioritize positive gaps from Most Inspirational to Fairly Interesting.
3. For each gap you identified, fill out the form in Appendix E.

CHAPTER SIX

Step Four—Your Fulfillment Plan™

The victory of success is half won when one gains the habit of setting goals and achieving them. Even the most tedious chore will become endurable as you parade through each day convinced that every task, no matter how menial or boring, brings you closer to fulfilling your dreams.

OG MANDINO, MOTIVATIONAL AUTHOR AND SPEAKER

There is nothing more unfortunate than to be inspired by a great vision, to clearly see the treasure that could be yours, but not to act upon the opportunity. The success you have experienced in life thus far is based not only on your ability to analyze a situation and dream big, but also on your willingness to act.

The work you have done up to this point gives you a clear map of what you need to do. You have consolidated your entire picture—your current lifestyle, your vision for your future, the legacy you want to leave—into one coherent vision. You are aware of all of your investments and their legal structures and whether they fit your Strategy Filter. You have prioritized your gaps, and new possibilities have arisen based on what your advisors have learned about you. Now it is time to act on those visions by implementing the strategies to close the gaps.

Your Fulfillment Plan™

A good Fulfillment Plan incorporates all the work you've done thus far into a detailed action checklist to ensure that you act on every intention. Unlike a lone advisor executing a single strategy, this Fulfillment Plan is a holistic blueprint for attaining all your life and financial goals. Often, financial plans assume that someone on your advisory team is implementing various strategies, but this takes the onus off you. Your Fulfillment Plan is set up

Your Fulfillment Plan is a blueprint for attaining your life and financial goals. as a contract between you and your individual advisors, specifying who is accountable for each task and the deadline for each one. Instead of trying to execute a good idea with only a vague sense of how to go about it, this Fulfillment Plan outlines specific criteria for the completion of each task.

The point of such an exhaustive plan is that, when it's complete, you'll be confident that your critical gaps are closed. You'll know that you are headed toward the visions that excite you, and you'll no longer have that nagging feeling that there might be some loose ends out there—loose ends that could turn into nightmares, as they did for Ned.

> Ned had experienced a disastrous and acrimonious first marriage followed by an intensely bitter divorce. Several years later, Ned was remarried to a delightful woman, Ella, who became his best friend and deepest love. This devoted couple came to us early in their marriage to discuss the financial structures that would be most appropriate for them and their now-blended families. In the course of our discussions, Ned told us that all assets were appropriately titled and confirmed the beneficiaries were correct.
>
> It was only when Ned died suddenly many years later that we looked at his life insurance policy and discovered that Ned's ex-wife was still listed as beneficiary.
>
> "It's not just about the money, though it did make things more difficult for a while," Ella told us later. "I just know that Ned would be upset to know that his ex-wife benefited from his death after all of the pain she had caused him and the children." A detailed Fulfillment Plan would have caught the error and saved Ned's family much heartache.
>
> **Ned's Blind Spot:** Ned didn't verify important details because he thought he remembered them correctly or assumed they had been handled, which proved disastrous.

What's Your Style?

We find that our clients have different styles when it comes to the fulfillment phase of their finances. Some are Do-It-Yourselfers who delegate only when absolutely necessary, such as when drafting legal documents for a living trust. Our Do-It-Yourselfers tend to place all of the action items on their own to-do list, not wanting to leave important tasks in others' hands. If they have time and tenacity, they can plow steadily through this extensive list, but many people find that trying to go it alone creates an unnecessary logjam and additional stress.

A second style we see is that of the Delegator. This person assigns all of the tasks from the action list to their advisors. The Delegator trusts everyone on the team to follow through on their tasks and to report back when the job is complete. This style distributes the work more evenly. We've seen two results of the Delegator approach. Sometimes, because the advisors are working independently, the results from different advisors are inconsistent, and each advisor tends to focus their actions toward their specific disciplines. Other Delegators create a coordinated team of advisors who work well together to ensure all details are handled.

The third style we have seen is that of the Collaborator. The Collaborator becomes a member of their team. Though many tasks are assigned to advisors, the Collaborator

- regularly confers with advisors, offering information and insight;
- constantly taps the brainpower of the advisors, encouraging them to come up with their most creative and appropriate solutions, and therefore gets the best they have to offer; and
- ensures, by remaining involved in the process, that the advisors stay focused on the Collaborator's unique goals and desires rather than getting sidetracked by less applicable strategies.

Can I Go It Alone?

No matter what your style, you will need various advisors to help you execute your Fulfillment Plan. In our culture, money remains a very private matter. Some say it is the last taboo subject for public discussion. A psychiatrist once claimed, "I can get a full sexual history in an hour, but it may take me weeks, months, or years before I can get the truth from someone about their money." It is considered in bad taste to discuss financial facts, so opening up your financial soul to a group of advisors may not sound particularly attractive.

Our culture also values independence and the ability to handle your own affairs. If you have the three Ts—time, talent, and temperament—and a strong desire to handle the ins and outs of your financial world, it is assumed that you should be smart enough to handle it yourself. However, if you are like most people, the myriad details and options of financial planning can be overwhelming or simply uninteresting. You may be able to find much more fulfilling ways to spend your time.

Some people don't like the idea of paying financial advisors for a job they feel they could do themselves, but an expert might know tips and strategies of which you were completely unaware. Besides, we all have blind spots when it comes to our own personal financial situation, and the "savings" you realize by not paying advisor fees could end up costing you more by having reduced performance in your investments or incurring avoidable income taxes. The benefits of excellent advice should always outweigh any fees.

If you're not sure where to get good help or whom you can trust, you're not alone. We often hear people complain about having to put up with underperforming advisors simply because they don't know how to find better ones. If you were seeing an underperforming physician, would you continue to visit them, or would you go without a doctor altogether? Neither of these options sounds very attractive. To find a good doctor, you would probably do what we recommend for finding good financial advisors: ask for referrals from friends or trusted professionals.

Picking the Players

Who should be on your team? First, you'll want the members of your team to have certain qualities. Your team cannot be as effective as it should be if all of its members do not possess the following qualities:

- **Trustworthiness:** It should be clear that they are acting for *your* benefit, not their own.
- **Reliability:** They should do what they say they will and within a reasonable timeline.
- **Good communication skills:** They should communicate clearly and make sure you understand recommendations, and they should listen and respond to your concerns and desires.
- **Innovation:** They should think up creative and innovative ways to address issues.

- **Expertise:** They should all be experts in their particular areas and be able to tailor their knowledge to your particular situation.

What team positions do you need to fill? Most people need

- an accountant, CPA, or tax preparer;
- an insurance professional;
- an investment advisor;
- a financial planner;
- an attorney for estate planning or business advice; and
- a wealth coach or team leader.

Depending on your particular situation, other advisors may also be valuable, such as a real estate broker or real estate attorney. One of your advisors may fill multiple roles; for example, your insurance professional may be able to handle your investments and financial planning. Although these advisors may be brilliant in their own disciplines, it will take some coordination to get them operating effectively as a team. Your team needs a leader. Who will that be?

If you are comfortable in that role, you are the logical person to lead this team. You know your advisors, you are aware of their strengths and weaknesses, and you are the one paying for their services. You are the person who can authorize them to share information or collaborate on certain tasks, and you have the power to approve or disapprove any decision. Especially on a newly formed team, your advisors are likely to be most responsive to you.

However, team leadership can also be a shared responsibility. Choosing one of your advisors as a co-leader is often an effective way to keep the team coordinated and running smoothly. In selecting a co-leader, consider which of your advisors has experience working with or leading multi-disciplinary teams, who has the broadest view of your total financial picture, and who is the most accessible and responsive.

If you are uncomfortable leading your team or sharing leadership, or if you simply do not have the time to do so, we still strongly urge you not to leave your team leaderless. Appoint one of your trusted advisors as your wealth coach or team leader and let the other team members know that he or she is empowered to coordinate the work of the Fulfillment Plan on your behalf.

A financial team or personal CFO allows you to spend your valuable time and energy elsewhere.

Does having a team seem unrealistic? You may think that you don't have enough money to warrant a team of advisors, or that you have too much money to trust others to make decisions for you. We have found that the vast majority of our clients, no matter their situation, benefit from a coordinated team working on their behalf. Working with a good financial team allows you to spend your time and energy elsewhere and makes the process exciting rather than exhausting.

How about a Personal CFO?

In recent years, many people have discovered the benefits of another position: a personal chief financial officer (CFO). This position has been given various titles, including wealth coach, lead advisor, or advisor quarterback, but they are all essentially the same position. The concept is similar to an agent or manager that an athlete or entertainer might hire: this person will oversee your financial affairs, coordinate your financial advisors, and keep track of all activities. Some professionals are specifically in the personal CFO or wealth coach business. For example, The Legacy Companies, LLC in Boston has a national network of what it has titled Legacy Wealth Coaches. Your personal CFO's purpose is to focus on your vision and goals, then make sure that your cash flow, assets, and financial structures remain suitable for your vision as it evolves.

To be effective, personal CFOs and wealth coaches should have comprehensive financial management as their core business model. They should have systems to do this type of work and their services should be fee-based. Certain qualities make a professional personal CFO more effective. He or she should be an independent thinker, have a broad perspective, be a good listener, be your advocate in helping you get what you want, be well organized, and have been doing this type of work for some years. You need to have total faith that this person will consistently act in your best interests. You may choose your current CPA, your investment advisor, or your financial planner for this position, or you may bring someone new to your team who has the skills and experience to be a personal CFO.

Who Needs a Personal CFO?

In today's busy world, people want more control over their time, whether it be to concentrate on their careers or to enjoy their favorite activities. At the same time, they don't want to miss any financial opportunities. So, although many people *could* be their own personal CFO, you may prefer to concentrate on what you do best and enjoy most. The financial world is complex and always changing, and it's not easy to keep up with new products and opportunities coming onto the market, but this is a CFO's job. A personal CFO stays in tune with new opportunities and changing markets and can thoroughly scrutinize opportunities their clients find. Since they are aware of their clients' unique Strategy Filters, personal CFOs can quickly discern if an opportunity is worth pursuing. If a new tax law is issued, a personal CFO can explain which aspects of it will apply to the client. As Hugh discovered, the coordination of all the parts of the financial picture can be smooth when a thoroughly competent personal CFO holds the reins.

Hugh had created a nice lifestyle for himself and his family. His business had done well and he had invested wisely over the years. However, it seemed that he never had a moment's rest from the responsibilities associated with managing his success. He always had something to worry about or deal with: a letter from the IRS saying there was an error with penalties owed on one of the many tax returns he had to file, a brokerage statement showing a precipitous drop in value, constant phone calls from tenants of a rental property, and e-mails of insurance quotes. Even on vacation, Hugh was more concerned about finding a place that had Internet access and cell phone coverage than a site with beautiful views and nice amenities.

After one vacation, Hugh's family was recalling how great it had been to see the whales playing in the water from the balcony of their room. Hugh was struck by the fact that he had no recollection of this—all he could remember was a lengthy conversation with his broker regarding the latest securities for his portfolio.

At that moment, Hugh decided to do for himself what he had done for his business when it had grown to a certain size. He would hire a CFO, only this CFO would coordinate and oversee his personal finances. He wrote a job description for his personal CFO: must be conversant with all family assets to help make decisions as necessary; must act as a lead advisor, coordinating the accounting and legal work needed to keep things running smoothly; must coordinate a team of advisors and field questions when necessary; must hire and oversee property management teams for real estate. Hugh also listed qualities he sought in this person: someone responsive, intelligent, and able to understand his vision and core values. The process of finding just the right person took a while. After interviewing CPAs, financial planners, attorneys, brokers, and life coaches, Hugh found an advisor, Tom, who was everything he wanted.

Six months after hiring his new personal CFO, Hugh joined his family at their vacation home on the coast.

"The mail came and I had a letter from the IRS about a deal I only vaguely remembered, a notice from an insurance company, and some bank statements that seemed off. Instead of stressing, I faxed them to Tom, put on my flip-flops, and took my latte down to the beach. My family is amazed at the difference in me."

Hugh's Blind Spot: Like many successful people, Hugh believed that he needed to handle his financial affairs himself.

What to Expect from a Personal CFO

Your personal CFO, lead advisor, or wealth coach should have a system for

- determining your vision, values, and goals—the guideposts of your financial management;
- evaluating your current status and identifying any gaps in your current financial structure that don't meet your vision, values, and goals;
- overseeing the implementation of all the strategies you chose to close your gaps;
- monitoring and reporting on your progress toward accomplishing your desired outcomes; and
- keeping track of the ongoing evolution of your life's goals and the financial structures that support you.

What benefits should you receive?

- Confidence that all your financial details are handled within the context of your vision
- Freedom and time to do what you really enjoy and what is really important to you

- A system and team that allow you to make good decisions when opportunities present themselves
- A financial confidant to consult when you have to make a life decision with financial repercussions, or a financial decision with life repercussions

The Fulfillment Plan™ Itself

We cannot seek or attain health, wealth, learning, justice or kindness in general. Action is always specific, concrete, individualized, unique.

JOHN DEWEY, PHILOSOPHER AND PSYCHOLOGIST

Everything from "re-title vacation home into living trust" to "train Sally to manage rental properties" belongs in your Fulfillment Plan. Items such as "discuss trust with children" or "close excess cash accounts" might also be listed. Tasks as large as "put together a family foundation" or as small as "make extra key for new property manager" will be there, as well as some personal goals, such as "find a personal trainer and lower cholesterol by 20 percent by Christmas."

The document itself may take many forms, from a task sheet generated by project management software such as Microsoft Project to a handwritten itemized checklist, but it is always written down; it's never just verbal or kept in your head. A good plan's critical components are as follows:

1. **Specific tasks**

   "Form a foundation" is merely the heading of a series of tasks to be performed. Tasks under that heading might include
   - create foundation structure;
   - create foundation by-laws;
   - appoint board of directors;
   - create foundation mission statement; and
   - fund foundation.

2. **Specific task owners**

   Though several advisors on the team may assist with a particular task, one person must be in charge of it and accountable for its completion. This prevents misunderstandings, finger pointing, and details slipping through the cracks. However, never assign ownership without discussion. It may seem obvious that a particular advisor should own a certain task, but they may not have the time or expertise to be in charge. Also keep in mind that one advisor might charge much higher fees than another for completing the same task.

3. **Completion criteria**

   When is each task really done? For example, is the living trust complete when its paperwork is executed, or when all assets have been re-titled into it? What documentation is needed for proper re-titling? Is that documentation filed in a way that makes it accessible? If your tasks have been fully detailed, determining criteria for true completion is not difficult.

4. **Targeted completion dates**

   "As soon as possible" is not a valid date! Real dates keep the team on track and accountable. Estimated completion dates should be realistic and based on the complexity of the task, the workload of the task owner, and the completion of tasks that must come first (for example, a living trust must be created before assets can be re-titled into it).

5. **A method for tracking progress**

   Whether it is through monthly meetings, weekly conference calls, or computer-based systems, the team needs to convene periodically to report progress, discuss challenges, and seek one another's advice. Your Fulfillment Plan serves as the agenda for these meetings to keep them focused and efficient.

Does this seem like a lot of work? Your prior financial planning processes probably did not involve this level of detail and coordination. Like many people we see for the first time, you may feel that everything is already in place. While that may be true for you, we have yet to help a client audit his or her financial situation without finding something—often a very important something—that is incomplete.

Patrick and Joanna had been, for the most part, very conscientious about the fulfillment of their financial strategies. They had consolidated cash accounts, divested themselves of non-performing assets, and created a living trust. They had named a local professional as successor trustee of their living trust, which stipulated that certain assets would go to their children and the remainder would go into a charitable foundation after both Patrick and Joanna died. As years went by, the foundation itself was never fully discussed. There were no gifting guidelines, no governance documentation, and no family meetings to discuss the foundation or its operation.

When Patrick was diagnosed with rapidly advancing Alzheimer's, Joanna decided it would be prudent to introduce the children to their advisor and explain aspects of their estate plan. Because the family hadn't previously discussed these arrangements, the children had always assumed that they would inherit their parents' entire estate. Already emotionally distraught over their father's condition, they were even more upset to learn that the foundation would receive nearly 50 percent of the estate. Furthermore, when the dust settled around that issue, the beneficiaries of this foundation became the center of a heated debate. Patrick and Joanna had always felt strongly about preserving wildlife and natural habitats, but both of their children were adamant about giving to local charities. The family finally worked through a compromise and documented it, but the whole situation took its toll on Joanna.

"If we'd done this before, while Patrick was still healthy, it might have turned out differently," she told us. "I'm not sure whether I've done the right thing, but the children were so upset and I couldn't risk alienating them further. At least the foundation will do some part of what we intended." Had they completed work on their foundation and discussed their estate with their children years before, Patrick and Joanna's intentions for their legacy could have been fully met.

Patrick and Joanna's Blind Spot: Patrick and Joanna procrastinated in their estate planning because they assumed they had plenty of time.

A comprehensive Fulfillment Plan is all about ensuring that what you intend to happen actually happens. It's also about giving you a clear-cut method of knowing what plans are firmly in place and an action plan for tying up any loose ends. The Fulfillment Plan gives you a stable foundation for gaining confidence by ensuring that your gaps are being closed and that your vision is being pursued.

> A comprehensive Fulfillment Plan ensures that what you intend actually happens.

Our client Clara was a widow in her late sixties. She and her husband had built an estate worth over $6 million. She came to us six years after her husband had passed away to straighten out her finances.

During the discovery process, Clara was able to clearly identify her core values and vision for the future, and that clarity motivated her to act. The vision of the legacy she wished to leave was particularly clear and compelling: she wanted to leave her children empowered by her wealth and to leave money to her three favorite charities rather than having it eroded by taxes. This vision required putting a number of new structures in place, and she tackled her Fulfillment Plan with vigor. This vision had now become her mission.

As the Fulfillment Plan was being implemented, it was discovered that the bypass trust to be created at her husband's death had not been funded. Clara, like many people, did not know that after her husband's death there were things she needed to do. She quickly transferred the appropriate assets—$600,000—into the trust, which grew to $2.5 million by the time of her death and passed to her children's estate tax-free. She also implemented a 10-year QPRT (Qualified Personal Residence Trust), a vehicle that allowed the title of her residence to revert to her children tax-free if she survived through the 10-year period. She did survive, and the property passed on to her children at the time of her death. Additionally, she established an annual gifting program for her children and grandchildren.

Clara had several annuities in her investment portfolio that had tax-deferred interest. This income would always be ordinary taxable income, and Clara was in a high tax bracket. Clara realized that her annuities were the perfect assets to leave to the three charities she cherished. They would get 100 percent of the money and her estate would avoid all taxes on them.

Because of the strategies she implemented, Clara's estate was virtually tax-free at her death. Because her planning had been so thorough, she was able to leave the legacy she intended, and her heirs were spared the burden of untangling a complex and unwieldy portfolio.

Clara's Blind Spot: Clara assumed that all the details of her financial strategies had been handled by professionals, but hadn't verified that they were. She was surprised when the exemption trust wasn't funded.

Wouldn't you like to feel the kind of confidence Clara must have felt when all the details of her Fulfillment Plan were completed?

The difference between perseverance and obstinacy is that one comes from a strong will, and the other from a strong won't.

HENRY WARD BEECHER, THEOLOGIAN AND ABOLITIONIST

TAKING ACTION: Your Fulfillment Plan™

1. Review pages 68 to 69 and determine your style. Are you a Do-It-Yourselfer, a Delegator, or a Collaborator?
2. Read the material and fill out the form in Appendix F: Your Advisory Team. Fill the positions on your team with current advisors or referrals.
3. Determine whether you could benefit from a personal CFO by reviewing pages 72 to 75. For references, see Appendix F.
4. Create (or have someone else create) a detailed project plan to fulfill the actions required for your identified gaps (refer to pages 75 to 76). Schedule regular project meetings or calls until all items have been completed.

CHAPTER SEVEN

Step Five—On-Track Monitor™

Much good work is lost for the lack of a little more.

EDWARD HARRIMAN, RAILROAD EXECUTIVE

The key to any good plan is sustainability, but life isn't static, so how can strategies that are appropriate today be effective two decades, or even just two years, later? When you are focused on wealth's treasures, your financial plan is a process that evolves and expands over time, just as your life does. The facts of your life change and your vision grows as you discover new interests, and perhaps new life challenges. People and passions may move in and out of your life—the only constant is change.

Most people who have experienced a traditional financial planning process are relieved when it is done. Traditional annual reviews become routine, but beyond tweaking a few investments or strategy structures, nothing much happens during those annual reviews to ease any sense of discomfort. Therefore, the thought of returning year after year is not particularly inspiring.

A n On-Track Monitor meeting allows you to see how your finances are supporting your values, clarify what is important to you, and evaluate the relevance of the current strategies you are using to pursue your dreams.

Planning that emphasizes your wealth's treasures doesn't focus merely on your financial data; it focuses on *you* and how to get you where you really want to be. Because of this focus, most of our clients find the initial process, from discovery all the way through to Fulfillment Plan, to be invigorating rather than painful or burdensome. They actually look forward to their regular reviews, which we call On-Track Monitor meetings. These sessions are opportunities to see how their current financial structure is supporting their core values and purpose. We clarify what is important to them and make sure that all strategies continue to be relevant to achieving their goals and aspirations.

Dust Off Your Vision

Life is a process of becoming, a combination of states we have to go through.
Where people fail is that they wish to elect a state and remain in it. This is a
kind of death.

ANAÏS NIN, AUTHOR

How does an On-Track Monitor meeting differ from a traditional review?
First of all, just as a quality discovery process was the cornerstone of your
original overall plan, discovery is an important part of determining whether
your plan is on track. At this stage, we call it "discovery light," because you've
already done much of the heavy lifting and important soul-searching. However, it is important to revisit your previously stated desires and vision for
two reasons: first, to verify that they still hold the same importance to you,
and that they are still relevant; and second, to remind you and your advisors
of the vision that is at the core of your financial plan. At review time, you
will be able to set new goals, track progress on current goals, and delete goals
that are no longer relevant. The process allows you to create a stable foundation, frees you from stress and worry, and liberates you to think creatively
about the present and future, like our clients Sam and Sally.

> Sam and Sally had already been through plenty of traditional planning sessions when
> they first came to us. They found it hard to believe that they would learn anything
> new or discover additional tasks that they needed to accomplish. They came to us
> because, despite all of their planning, they still could not relax about their financial
> situation.
>
> As we led them through our process, Sam and Sally found the certainty about
> their finances that had been missing, and were able to rediscover dreams they'd had
> when they first met, 27 years before. They started a notebook together containing
> the dreams they had for their family and community, and they allowed their imagi-
> nations to run free for the first time in decades. They brought their notebook to their
> On-Track Monitor meetings to keep their vision fresh and in focus.
>
> Over the years, Sam and Sally moved closer to their goal of a major philan-
> thropic gift. Out of the blue, another event took priority in their lives: their daughter
> gave birth to triplets—three new baby girls in a household that already had three
> children. As excited as Sam and Sally were, they were equally frustrated to be 3,000
> miles away—their daughter lived in Florida and they were in California. Plane rides

back and forth were exhausting, and they knew their daughter needed more help than they could provide from across the country.

One evening, while reviewing their notebook, they had a thought. The money earmarked for philanthropy did not have to be used for that purpose, and they knew from their latest On-Track Monitor meeting that there was excess in their philanthropy account. Sally did some research and found a 15-acre property in Florida with a private beach. They realized they had more than enough savings to purchase the property and build a house for themselves, one for their daughter's family, and even a guesthouse for a live-in nanny.

Though Sam and Sally were cautious in suggesting the idea to their daughter and her husband, the young, besieged parents were tearfully grateful and enthusiastic about the plan. The land was purchased and subdivided (generating enough funds to re-establish their philanthropic account), and Sam and Sally moved into an apartment in Florida for the winter while their new home was being designed and built. An excellent example of rediscovering wealth's treasures!

Even if you are on the right track, you will get run over if you just sit there.
WILL ROGERS, PHILOSOPHER AND HUMORIST

Another Gift of Confidence

Once you have clarified your vision, established your Red Dot, identified your gaps and strategies to eliminate them, and developed a system to track your progress, you will begin to feel confident that your financial picture will support your dreams as well as your needs. This confidence can be the platform that allows you to look beyond yourself and discover the contributions you might make to others. For many people, the ability to make a major contribution is the most precious hidden treasure of wealth.

TAKING ACTION: On-Track Monitor™

1. Review and revise the visions, values, and goals you created during your original discovery process. Include your mission or purpose, if you have developed one.

2. Ask yourself the following questions:
   - Which still apply today?
   - How have they changed?
   - Have new horizons appeared?
   - Have the planned strategies been completed and adjusted each year so that they work as intended?

PART THREE

Contribution

Making A Difference

Contribution (n): influence, input, role, involvement, say, impact, aid, support; donation, gift, giving, payment, subsidy, backing, supply, provision

Since 1901, the Nobel Prize has honored men and women from all corners of the globe for outstanding achievements in physics, chemistry, medicine, literature, and work toward peace. The foundation for the prize was laid in 1895, when Alfred Nobel wrote his last will, leaving much of his wealth to its establishment.

But who was Alfred Nobel? He is a perfect example of someone who woke up to the power of contribution.

Alfred was a scientist, inventor, entrepreneur, author, and pacifist. He successfully produced a material he patented as dynamite in 1867, which drastically reduced the cost of blasting rock, drilling tunnels, building canals, and many other forms of construction work. Alfred was also a skillful entrepreneur and businessman, and he turned his dynamite patent into a fortune.

While dynamite had many good uses, it was also dangerous; in fact, it killed Alfred's brother Emil in 1864. One day in Paris in 1888, Alfred opened up his newspaper and was surprised to find his own obituary. His brother Ludwig had just died, and the paper mistakenly ran an obituary for Alfred instead. In it, he was called "The Merchant of Death" because of the dangers of dynamite, and he did not like what he read. From then on, Alfred decided he would use his resources to champion human achievement, and when he died in 1896, he bequeathed the bulk of his fortune to create annual prizes honoring ingenuity in the five fields mentioned above.

The odd coincidence of reading his own obituary and peering into his legacy before he actually died gave Alfred Nobel a rare opportunity. He was able to change his legacy and make a significant contribution that lives on to this day.

While the Alfred Nobel legacy is on one end of the spectrum, consider the story of Frank Thomas, who made a big difference in others' lives with no significant financial resources. Frank was a lighthouse keeper with no children who, in his will, left three envelopes, each containing a letter and a few small items.

The first envelope contained $16.90 in cash and a letter to John Griffen:

Dear John,

Many years ago, before beginning work at the lighthouse, I was unemployed with a wife and young daughter to feed. I was down to my last few dollars. I went to the grocery store check-out stand and the total came to $16.90. I reached for my money, but it was gone. I was humiliated and heartbroken. I took my wife by the hand and started to leave when someone touched me and handed me the $16.90. John, that man was your late father. I was only one minute in his presence, but I will never forget him. He didn't have much either, but he had something I really admired. He had character. I've spent the last 50 years trying to pass on all he showed me in that single encounter. John, I am now returning the money your father gave me long ago. Now you carry the baton.

Sincerely,

Frank Thomas

John returned to his auto repair shop and encountered a woman whose car he had repaired. He presented her with a bill totaling $400, and she panicked over the expense. She said she only had $200, but could make payments over time. Inspired by his gift from Frank, John said he wouldn't charge her for labor and would accept her $200 as full payment. On her way home, the woman, full of gratitude, felt compelled to share her few remaining dollars with a homeless man living on the street.

Frank's second envelope was for Donna Wilkens. He left her a dried flower and the following note:

Dearest Mrs. Wilkens,

I never thanked you for the difference you made in my life. Many years ago, I was watching from the lighthouse the day you lost your daughter in the drowning accident at the beach. What a sad day it was. You didn't notice me as I cried along with you. Oddly, I lost my own daughter not long after. She was my inspiration and my life, and her loss was more than I could accept. I became very bitter, life lost its luster, and as months passed by, the dark clouds stayed with me, hanging over me like a shadowy shroud. I was at my daughter's gravesite one day, and you came by and said "Beautiful day, isn't it?" and gave me a flower. I saw that you had dealt with your loss and were able to carry on. You were visiting your daughter's gravesite with flowers and a song in your heart, and your smile gave me the courage to go on. Your flower was a constant reminder to keep my head up, regardless of the storm. Thank you, Donna. I will give your daughter a hug and a kiss when I see her.

God Bless,

Frank Thomas

Donna Wilkens vowed to send condolence cards, sharing her experience of how she moved on in her life, to any parent who lost a child, even if she didn't know them personally.

The third envelope contained a sea shell and a note for a man named Richard Marks.

Richard,

Your shell is the object I have valued most in my life. I felt that it was finally time to return it. You see, many years ago, this shell belonged to you. You were young, recently married, and hopelessly in love. You were looking at this shell and left it on the log where you were sitting. You didn't see me, but I couldn't help noticing you and your wife. How happy and dedicated to each other you and your young bride were. You made me quite envious. My own marriage was fading fast and you two sent my mind racing back to a time when we were completely in love and very happy. As I watched you, I heard a phrase that I had forgotten how to say. "I love you." I heard your words every time I looked at that shell I captured from the log. It gave me the courage to swallow my pride. I went to my wife, said I was sorry for the way things had turned out, and told her how much I loved her. My life became so much more enjoyable after that. Thank you for your example and showing me how powerful a few well-placed kind words can be.

Frank Thomas

Richard was reminded of the love and tenderness that he and his wife had once shared. He called his attorney to cancel an appointment he'd made to discuss a possible divorce and vowed to restore that original love and tenderness.

In each of these cases, not only was the recipient inspired by Frank's small gift, but it inspired their actions toward others as well—a true legacy of making a difference in people's lives.

Whether you contribute to others during your lifetime or at the end of your life, and whether your gift is large or small, giving to others creates a feeling of a life well lived that is hard to come by in any other manner.

CHAPTER EIGHT

Legacy Planning

The only wealth which you will keep forever is the wealth you have given away.
ATTRIBUTED TO MARCUS AURELIUS, ROMAN EMPEROR AND PHILOSOPHER

We touched on the idea of legacy planning in earlier chapters, but because your contribution to your family, your community, and the world via your legacy can be one of wealth's greatest treasures, we'll look at it in more depth. A must-read for anyone serious about creating a legacy and a life of significance is *Values-Based Estate Planning* by Scott C. Fithian.

Legacy *versus* Estate

First, to be clear, estate planning and legacy planning are not synonymous. Estate planning is a tactical strategy. Specifically, it involves instructions on who gets which assets and what strategies to use to minimize taxes when assets are transferred. Estate planning is critical. People often don't realize the problems caused by the lack of good estate planning. Estate planning attorneys and advisors can recite a litany of horror stories about families that splintered after mom and dad died because the estate was mishandled. So why do so few people have current estate plans? One of the final gifts you can leave your children and family members is an estate plan that does its job. Be kind to those you leave behind. They will already have their grief to contend with; don't give them a pile of unresolved financial issues to tackle as well.

Despite all the ways an estate plan can help, there are some things that traditional estate planning may not do:

- Delve into the reasons behind your giving to heirs or to charity.
- Ensure that your giving is aligned with your core values.
- Seek solutions for problems your gifting might cause for recipients.
- Take into account the valuable intangible assets you have to share.

Because traditional estate planning does not address these issues, it's not uncommon for people to end up feeling uneasy despite having well-constructed, technically sound estate plans. A survey sponsored by the Allianz Life Insurance Company asked 2,500 people about the large wealth transfers they anticipated over the next 30-plus years. It found that people aged 40 and older ranked money last on their list of important estate issues. Ahead of it, they listed sharing values and life lessons, conveying final instructions and wishes to be fulfilled, and distributing personal possessions that have emotional value.[1]

Your Legacy: More than Money

Though you may have created a detailed will or a living trust and transferred your assets in the most tax-efficient manner, can you really say that your estate plan captures your deepest intentions, hopes, and desires? You may worry about your children's ability to deal with the wealth that you will leave them, or whether a charity will be in a position to receive and wisely handle the amount you left it.

Legacy planning differs from traditional estate planning in many ways. The word legacy is defined as "that which is bequeathed to future generations" or "that which is handed down to posterity." You often hear the word legacy used to describe the impact, positive or negative, that a public figure has on history. Legacy planning encompasses much more than the material assets you will leave behind after your death. It's about your talents, values, passions, and wisdom. Legacy planning concentrates on the impact you would like to leave on your world. Your legacy is the fingerprints you leave behind for those you care about, the organizations you support, and the community in which you live.

Legacy planning also explores ways that you can begin leaving your desired impact today, rather than delaying it until after you are gone. It encourages you to work now to transfer to your heirs certain intangible assets such as your work ethic, honesty, integrity, decision-making methods, and core values. Without a deliberate structure to help future generations receive these very important intangibles while you are alive, they may disappear with your passing. Legacy planning also helps structure the transfer of tangible assets in ways that will not only minimize tax repercussions, but will also be optimally beneficial to heirs or charitable organizations.

True legacy planning hasn't yet become common in our culture. Many survivors of the Great Depression live with constant financial fear, so to them, considering what might be left to give away seems insignificant or unknowable. Even with sound traditional financial planning, most people feel uncertain about whether they will have enough money to live comfortably through their own lifetime, let alone have surplus to give away. Extensive, in-depth planning can seem to be a fruitless exercise if you feel that it involves planning to give away what you don't think you will have.

We say "wealth is more than money." When you realize that your wealth is made up of your experiences, wisdom, talents, and values, planning to transfer those valuable assets to others can be a very motivating and fulfilling exercise.

Many people have a strong sense of humility, and think that the only thing of worth they have to leave behind is what they have built financially. Some of our clients are veterans of World War II; they flew fighter planes and stormed the beaches of Normandy, yet they think of themselves as ordinary folks whose personal histories would not interest future generations. A brilliant client of ours, a businesswoman, was astonished when we told her how valuable it would be if she could offer her wisdom to other female entrepreneurs. Another client had never considered that the watercolors she had painted for fun over the years would be a precious legacy for her grandchildren. Humility often blinds people to how special they are and to the unique gifts that can make up their legacy. This is a common blind spot in legacy planning.

However, once our clients have resurrected the visions and passions that give vibrancy to their lives, once they feel confident about their financial abundance and surplus, and once they see that their Fulfillment Plan is coming to life, they discover the great joy that comes with distributing their wealth purposefully, creatively, and generously. They begin to recognize the value of their intangible assets and enjoy the process of incorporating them into their legacy.

Surplus wealth is a sacred trust which its possessor is bound to administer in his lifetime for the good of the community.

ATTRIBUTED TO ANDREW CARNEGIE, INDUSTRIALIST AND PHILANTHROPIST

Legacy planning begins with the process of discovery. You will fully understand your own core values, dreams, and passions, and after developing your Red Dot in Chapter Four, you will become confident and have clear information about your financial picture and the current and potential future surplus. Your vision is clear—you are ready to take action and make it a reality.

The "Heavenly Look Down"

Imagine yourself looking through the Pearly Gates at the earth below, seeing your family, your friends, and your community after you are gone. What is your vision of each loved one? What do you wish you had told them or taught them now that you see them without you? How have they used the money you left them? Is there something you could have done to positively affect your community during your lifetime? Is there something you wish you had left to benefit others? Taking a look at your legacy from this perspective can influence your actions and plans today.

Most people begin their legacy planning with their families. Anything beyond dividing your estate equally between your children is usually where conventional planning stops. Have you ever thought about the real legacy you would like to leave to those you love—children, dear friends, or other relatives? This brings to mind some stumbling blocks that will short-circuit the planning before it begins. We'll discuss the issues involving children and their inheritance in the next chapter. For now, let's examine common issues related to giving to those you care about.

Is it Really What They Want from Us?

Our client Charlie has parents who live across the country in Florida. He and his siblings made efforts to visit them regularly, but they especially looked forward to their annual reunion each spring. It included the entire family, a lively group of 37 people, including kids, grandchildren, and even one great-grandchild. For each reunion, Charlie's parents rented guesthouses nearby; the accommodations were packed and noisy and full of life. At the end of each reunion, Charlie's parents would have a festive catered luau. As his parents aged and became less healthy, these reunions grew particularly precious.

One year, Charlie's parents announced that they were not going to have the family reunion. "We're getting on," they said, "and we want to make sure that we have plenty to leave you when we die." Their children didn't understand. Their parents were very well off, and so were Charlie and his siblings. They didn't need the money.

The family was devastated, until it occurred to them that they could sponsor the reunion themselves, luau and all. So they did—and spent precious time with their parents.

While the parents started the tradition of yearly reunions and stopped because of the expense, the value of family togetherness was so strongly passed to the next generation that they made sure the reunions continued.

Charlie's Parents' Blind Spot: Charlie's parents believed that, above all, it is important to leave a financial inheritance to your children in lieu of spending money on them today.

What people want from us is not always what we think they want. We get ideas in our heads about what would be best for others, but sometimes we're wrong. Effective gifting should be a combination of giving what we want to give and what the recipient desires to receive.

Arthur had always been an American history buff, and collected books and memorabilia related to wars his country has fought. He knew that his son Ralph enjoyed history too, so he thought about purchasing a large collection to add to his estate for Ralph. Fortunately, Arthur mentioned this to Ralph, who said, "Dad, while I love history, I'd really rather know about your personal history and more about my grandparents. I'd like to have that for my kids when they grow up." Surprised yet flattered, Arthur called off his offer to purchase the collection and hired a personal historian to help him create a video about his life, his deceased wife's life, and some history of his forebears. He also had a family tree created that included the names of his young grandchildren. The project was not only a thrilling gift to his son but also an exciting endeavor that gave Arthur a new perspective on his life.

Arthur's Blind Spot: Arthur assumed he knew what Ralph would value and need in his inheritance, but he didn't talk with him about it. It was only after he spoke with his son that he discovered the kind of inheritance he would really treasure.

Do They Understand My Intentions?

> Our clients Andrea and Mark received an enormous windfall from their investments one year. Knowing that Andrea's brother, Tim, was not doing well financially, the couple decided to share their good fortune and help Tim pay off the large credit card debt he had accumulated. When they called and made the offer, Tim was hesitant but told them how much he needed to erase his debt. They wrote a check that night and sent it off to him.
>
> Oddly, their relationship with Tim became very strained after that. He rarely returned their phone calls and made excuses for avoiding family gatherings. It took two years before Tim revealed the problem: "When you gave me that money," Tim said, "I felt like you thought I was a loser and would never be able to get myself out of the jam I was in."
>
> **Andrea and Mark's Blind Spot:** Andrea and Mark assumed that if they helped someone with their financial problems, that person would appreciate it.

Ouch! The moral of this story is *not* that you should hesitate to give when you feel moved to do so. The moral is that, prior to giving, you need to talk with the recipient, explain the loving intentions behind your gift, and allow them to express what they would really like from you.

Is the Timing Right?

Deciding when to give doesn't just depend on your plans; the timing is also important to your recipient.

> Agnes was in her seventies when we first met her. She was a skilled artist, and the sale of her watercolors had made her a wealthy woman. She loved mentoring budding artists, so she taught at a local community college. In one of her classes, she met Ken, a very talented and passionate young man.
>
> "I'd like to leave a substantial amount to him in my will," she told us. "It will allow him to pursue what he was meant to do." Agnes felt wonderful about this decision, and despite keeping in close contact with Ken, never informed him about it.
>
> Over the next 15 years, their friendship grew. With a family of four to support, Ken was never able to fully pursue his art. He maintained his 9-to-5 job as a department store manager and, in his rare free moments, produced beautiful paintings that Agnes adored.
>
> Then he suddenly died of an aneurism.

"What was I thinking?" she said to us after his death. "I didn't need the money. If I had given it to him 15 years ago, so much of his wonderful work would be with us today, and he would have made enough from the sale of his work to give security to his family."

Agnes's Blind Spot: Agnes never considered giving money during her life-time because the standard practice is to give it upon death.

Social Capital

When defining your legacy, you should also consider the impact you would like to have on your community or the world. People often create this legacy by making contributions to the causes that inspire them. Many people think the title "philanthropist" is reserved for the Rockefellers, Gateses, Carnegies, or Fords—the ultrawealthy. But the definition of philanthropist is someone who donates money, time, goods, or effort to a cause that promotes the public good. By that definition, most people are philanthropists.

In fact, the term "involuntary philanthropist" has been coined to apply to all taxpayers. Taxes promote the public good, so the term "social capital" applies to the part of an estate that will go to taxes—unless you do something to change where it goes. The idea of a zero-tax estate plan is based on the notion that we can control our social capital. We have the choice of giving our taxes either to Uncle Sam or to the charities we want to support.

How to Give

Most people do not come from wealthy families who mentored them in philanthropy. Many simply donate to the cause *du jour* with no clear sense of their contribution's effectiveness. They are checkbook philanthropists who sprinkle small donations over a variety of organizations.

As an alternative, many people turn to committed giving, often in the form of tithing. The concept of tithing is to give a percentage, usually 10 percent, of your income. Some religious groups promote tithing to the church, some individuals practice tithing based on the philosophy that giving is good for the soul, and some feel that generous giving will attract blessings to the giver.

More and more of our clients are finding satisfaction in inspired giving by making contributions based on a passion or special cause. Because this form of giving is so exciting, the involvement of inspired givers often reaches beyond cash donations. They might become personally active in their favorite causes, they might become creative about what they offer the cause, and sometimes they desire to leave part of their assets as a legacy to that cause.

Are you inspired by a special cause? If you aren't sure, try answering these questions:

What is your personal passion? *Marcy loves animals and is a major sponsor of her local zoo's annual fundraiser.*

What really annoys you? What problems would you like to help solve? What good acts would you like to encourage? Pay attention to news stories and anecdotes and observe what annoys you or moves you to tears. *Stephanie read an article about emancipated foster youths who had no money to go to college. The article affected her so powerfully that she decided to set up a college scholarship fund. So far, she has sponsored eight students, three of whom have already graduated.*

What life experiences have powerfully influenced you and might propel you to action? *Tony had a very close relationship with his grandmother, so he feels very passionately about taking care of the elderly. He gives a large portion of his donations to Meals on Wheels and loves visiting "his" seniors when he delivers meals to them once a week.*

What do you value? What is important to you? Look at the events in your life, positive and negative, and see how they shaped your values. *Don and Beth had several rough spots in their marriage that could have resulted in divorce. They chose the path of commitment and loyalty and today they remain happily married. They started and funded The Marriage Enhancement Project at their church as a way to help all the marriages in their church community become stronger and more enjoyable.*

What charitable organizations inspire you with their work? *Craig was impressed that Sierra Forever Families provides permanent families for older children in foster care, which saves them from being on their own at 18. He set up an endowment fund in the agency's name and offers his time to recruit prospective adoptive families.*

What is your vision for the world? What would you like to do to move that vision forward? *A client of ours is an environmentalist who wished to leave local parkland for future generations. He bought several beautiful undeveloped acres within the city and planted additional trees and wildflowers on them over the years. When he dies, the property will be left to the Parks and Recreation District.*

As the vision of your unique legacy becomes clear, a way to achieve your legacy will become apparent. As you begin to see the effects of your legacy on your community and your loved ones, you'll discover the secret we're trying to impart: the person who receives the most from generous giving is always you, the giver.

TAKING ACTION: Legacy Planning

1. Reread the "heavenly look down" described on page 92. Use your imagination, and record your thoughts on what you would like to see.
2. Write down the names of all of your loved ones. Think of each individually, and what you would like to leave them. Consider both tangible and intangible assets you can offer them, and the unique issues you should consider for each.
3. Using the questions on pages 102 to 103, think about the legacies you might leave to your community. Write down any ideas about what you'd like to contribute now or after death.
4. Take these lists to your financial planner or other trusted advisor. Find out what needs to be done to turn your desired legacies into a reality.
5. Add the action steps from #4 to your Fulfillment Plan.

CHAPTER NINE

Empowering Children

Property left to a child may soon be lost, but the inheritance of virtue—a good name, an unblemished reputation—will abide forever. If those who are toiling for wealth to leave their children would but take half the pains to secure for them virtuous habits, how much more serviceable would they be. The largest property may be wrested from a child, but virtue will stand by him to the last.

UNKNOWN

The Silver Spoon

It is estimated that there are now more than four million children of American millionaires. According to a study by the Boston College Social Welfare Research Institute, approximately $40 trillion will be passed down to children of millionaires between 2002 and 2052.[1] A survey by wealth research company Prince & Associates found that most of today's millionaires plan to leave at least 75 percent of their estates to their children.[2] The number is highest for families with households worth $25 million or more, discrediting the widely held notion that wealthier families are more likely to leave a greater share to charity.

One of the strongest motivations for building wealth is "creating a better life for our family." People want to provide security and opportunities for their loved ones that they might not have experienced themselves as children. They don't want their children or grandchildren to struggle as they struggled, or to have to work as hard as they worked. They're willing to sacrifice so their heirs don't have to make similar sacrifices.

However, after amassing significant financial holdings, the vast majority of our clients say that passing this wealth on to the next generations has become a huge concern. They recognize that some of the struggles they've helped their offspring avoid are the very struggles that build character and create self-confidence. They see that children who have never worked for money often don't value it, and even if they do appreciate money, they usually don't know how to handle it. But is money itself really the culprit?

Charity begins at home—as do frugality, courtesy, perseverance, honesty, work ethic, gratitude, education, and generosity. Too often, parents and grandparents who are focused on amassing wealth are living according to these qualities, but are not teaching them to their offspring. Especially in recent decades, the emphasis has been on giving children opportunities: the best schools, tutoring, extra-curricular lessons, personal coaches, and travel, among others. It's hard to avoid following the same path, but when every child in your fourth grader's class is taking ballet and tennis lessons, owns a horse, and has extravagant birthday parties, your child may easily slip into an attitude of entitlement.

These activities teach children about wealth's privileges, but not its responsibilities or real treasures. Privilege doesn't teach children to be good stewards of the financial assets you wish to leave them, and it doesn't teach children the basic values they need in order to live fulfilling and productive lives. Rather than feeling gratitude for the special opportunities they receive, some children begin to take such things for granted. Because they lack appreciation for their blessings, they are often unhappy.

Without basic values in place, some children will use inherited wealth to self-destruct rather than to find happiness and success. Too often, even large inheritances never make it past the second or third generation because that generation is ill equipped to handle the responsibility.

In her book *Navigating the Dark Side of Wealth*, Thayer Willis describes many individuals who have inherited large sums of money. In many of these cases, the inheritors struggle to find their purpose in life and feel that they were never given an instruction manual for managing the money they inherited.

One young woman inherited several million dollars during her second year of college. She stayed in college because her father (who had never graduated from high school) claimed that a college education was essential for gaining the respect of others. After graduation, however, she couldn't find a career or interest that made her feel successful. She found her managers too difficult and demanding or the work boring and tedious. Now in her late twenties, she has gone back to school, still trying to find her niche. Hers is an all-too-common story.

What Old Money Knew

Some of the moneyed dynasties in the U.S. were more successful than others at combining wealth and values in their legacy. The Kennedys and Rockefellers are both known for instilling in their offspring a commitment to community service and charitable giving. In years past, boarding schools for wealthy children prepared them for the roles they would be expected to fill in future years, emphasizing the value of hard work, learning to overcome obstacles, and developing leadership skills. These values were taught in the classroom, during sports, and through community service projects that some schools required for graduation.

Many schools for wealthy youngsters have changed. They are now more like country clubs than training academies, and many old-money families no longer mentor their children as they did in past generations. Jamie Johnson, an heir of the Johnson & Johnson family, produced a documentary, *Born Rich,* that looks into the thoughts and attitudes of super-wealthy young men and women. Approaching his twenty-first birthday, the date on which he would inherit his portion of the family fortune, Jamie set out to understand how young people born into wealth feel about their place in a society that esteems meritocracy. Many interviewees said that their families never discussed money; some only learned the extent of their wealth through the media. Several ended up with severe drug or alcohol problems, and many, as Thayer Willis's inheritors reported, felt a total lack of purpose and struggled with their sense of identity.

What Do You Really Want Them to Inherit?

Concerns about gifting money and assets to family are valid. Will money destroy personal ambition or motivation? Will it add fuel to existing bad habits? Will one child feel less appreciated or loved based on comparative gifts? Like the families in *Born Rich*, too many parents are afraid to tackle these issues via deliberate communication, so their concerns only grow. However, if you consider that the wisdom you've acquired is a valuable asset worth sharing, the process becomes more inviting, and you can focus on becoming a positive mentor to those who will inherit your wealth.

When people really focus on wealth's treasures, they embrace a fresh perspective and develop a number of creative ways to mentor those who will inherit their wealth.

> Max takes his grandchildren to visit his various businesses. He explains what they do and how they got started. He tells them (in age-appropriate terms) about the businesses' milestones and the difficulties they've overcome, and he talks about the people who helped along the way and the lessons he learned from them.
>
> Sharon starts her children with an investment fund as soon as they reach high school. She joins each child for their quarterly meeting with the financial advisor to help make decisions and track progress. She also brings her children to her own financial planning sessions so they can see how she deals with her own investments.

There are myriad creative ways to be a financial mentor. The point to remember is that your legacy can be more than cash and assets—your wisdom and insight are much more valuable to your heirs.

Is It Ever Too Late?

Many of our clients didn't consider the potential problems that could arise from passing their assets on to their children until much later in life.

> Our new clients Karla and Kyle had done extensive estate planning before coming to us. Nevertheless, after we asked them to think about the potential treasures of their wealth, they realized that there were much more satisfying ways to resolve the concerns they had about leaving vast sums of money to their son, Mike.
>
> At 32, Mike was still fairly naïve and irresponsible about money. He had always spent his full allowance immediately, and when he entered the work world, he did the same with his paychecks. Though he seemed to have his father's knack for making money, he was unable to save or invest and had little to show for it.
>
> Concerned that Mike would run through his inheritance as quickly as his paycheck, Karla and Kyle's original estate plan included a carefully restrictive trust arrangement that would allow Mike very limited, incremental access to the estate; however, this solution felt uncomfortable to all three of them.
>
> When they took the perspective that part of their legacy was to empower Mike, Karla and Kyle realized that they would like to leave their son with the stable and comfortable relationship with money that they had. They decided to give Mike a

substantial portion of his inheritance now within a structured mentoring process. Mike was responsible for finding a financial advisor, and the three of them attended planning sessions together.

Mike became a dedicated student of the process, studying markets and doing research on his own. He even began to save and invest from his own earnings. Family dinners became lively discussions of effective financial strategies, expanding into the value of philanthropy. Mike no longer felt stressed and embarrassed by his financial naïveté, and Karla and Kyle felt the satisfaction of giving their son a true legacy—that of self-confidence and self-reliance.

Karla and Kyle's Blind Spot: Karla and Kyle treated Mike as though he had no capacity to deal with financial matters.

Is it ever too late? Probably not, but children who inherit wealth with no guidance, structure, or value system will certainly have a much rougher time building the skills and confidence to manage money. Today is the day to begin teaching your children, regardless of their age.

Teaching Children Skills and Values for Managing Wealth

Educating children about money should be undertaken like any other form of education: teach a lesson, give an assignment, and discuss the assignment after it has been completed. Your child may not grow up to be a financial wizard, but he or she needs to have basic competence and understanding to make judgments on financial matters. The best approach is assigning your children a variety of hands-on activities so that they can test their decisions, make some mistakes, and receive guidance and feedback.

Here are some activities you can use:

- Set up a savings account in your child's name and let them decide what portion of their allowance or income will go into it regularly.
- Open a mutual fund account with a company that has numerous investment choices. Your child can read about their choices, help decide where their money will be invested, and then help track their returns over time.
- Encourage your child to watch news on the economy from around the world with you. Discuss with them what they think it means.

Raising motivated, self-confident children seems to take a lot of work, and sometimes it's easier to just do things for them than to train and encourage them to do things for themselves. Consistently doing things for children rather than letting them make their own mistakes disables them and prevents them from becoming self-sufficient, sometimes for life.

> Arnold Schwarzenegger, actor and governor of the state of California, was raised in post–World War II Austria, where resources were scarce. Although now very wealthy, he insists his children be responsible and self-reliant. They do their own laundry despite the fact that the family could easily afford to pay someone to do it for them. If he finds the children have left lights on in their bedrooms, wasting energy, he removes the bulbs from all of the fixtures in that room for a period of time. Schwarzenegger insists that his children understand the value of money and resources as well as learn how to take care of themselves.

Children are not lazy. They enjoy learning to do things for themselves and feel good about it, though at any given moment they may prefer playing a video game to helping dad fix something around the house. Generations ago, it was common for children to work side by side with their elders to learn life skills: how to bake a pie, plow a field, or run a business. But in the hectic pace of today's world, many parents have lost that focus on mentoring their children.

The young people in the film *Born Rich* did not need to work to support themselves, but those who had experienced hard work in some form tended to exhibit higher self-esteem and more clarity of purpose than those who had not. It's a liberating feeling to know that you can work hard to make something happen or produce something of value. A child who knows how to work for what he or she wants is powerful and will become a productive adult.

How do you begin a self-reliance program for the children in your life—your own children, but also your grandchildren, godchildren, nieces and nephews, and young friends? Often you can develop creative ideas by thinking about your own childhood and remembering the experiences that taught you self-reliance. Here are some suggestions to get you started:

- Teach children to be self-sufficient by letting them figure out ways to earn money to buy items they want. Let them work to earn money rather than give it to them.

- Depending on their ages, give them chores to do at home and pay them an allowance, or encourage them to get summer jobs or work in the family business.
- Encourage them to pursue fun projects of their own, such as writing a book, learning a sport, or building a dog house.
- Let them do things on their own and make some mistakes. Know, and let them know, too, that their first attempts will not be perfect.
- Increase their responsibilities, or let go of the reins occasionally and let them take charge where they can.
- Ask them to do things for others who may not be able to do for themselves: mow an elderly neighbor's lawn, for example, or babysit for a single parent who needs extra help.
- Encourage creative thinking and alternative problem solving. Children are natural "outside the box" thinkers.

Involving Your Children in Their Inheritance

Family discussions about household finances and expenses are rare in this country, but they can be extremely valuable. Many parents are uncomfortable disclosing financial details to their children. They may be concerned that their children will expect more than they are receiving or, just the opposite, that they will worry about financial issues at too early an age. Whatever the reason, the taboo of speaking about money sends a message that money is too complicated for them to understand, and that they are not in control of their financial future.

Beyond discussing day-to-day finances, a detailed discussion of expectations—what you will provide financially to your children and what you expect your children to provide to you—is also critical. At a young age, this could involve giving them an allowance for clothes or toys or technology, and telling them that anything above that amount will have to come from their own pockets. When your child reaches driving age, it may involve providing them with a car but making them pay for gas, maintenance, and insurance. Later, you will need to discuss whether you will pay for college or graduate school, and whether you expect them to earn scholarships or pay for their own room and board. After college, discuss what you will do to help them get started, such as paying for health insurance, providing career counseling, helping with a downpayment on a house, or helping them pay for a wedding. And if you offer to pay for their wedding, you should also discuss whether you would pay for a second wedding.

During these discussions, it is important to remind yourself and your children that these decisions are unique to your family. Just because Susie's dad will buy her a new convertible for her sixteenth birthday or John's family sent him to Europe after college does not mean that you will do similar things. Explain your decisions and the core values that underlie them.

In his book *Family Wealth*, James Hughes says that strong families have specific qualities. One is good communication, especially concerning money. The most committed families not only have open discussions about money, but they hold meetings to discuss the goals and wishes of the parents and children. These communication experiences create a foundation for more complex conversations later in life, such as discussing the parents' estate plan. Parents who pursue these steps are dedicated to doing whatever it takes to create a legacy that will keep their family in harmony.

> We conducted a family meeting for one of our clients who had two children. Their older son was financially competent and successful, while their younger son was financially incompetent and poor—a discrepancy not unusual in families today. Like most parents, our clients felt they should not punish their older son for his success and leave the entire inheritance to his brother. The parents equated money with love and fairness, and wanted to show both children how important they were to them through their estate plan. Because they all communicated candidly during the family meeting, the parents came to understand that their older son was worried about having to take care of his brother after they were gone. He was able to tell them that he wanted them to leave $50,000 to each of his two children and the rest to his brother's trust so that he would be relieved of the burden of his financial well-being. The family's love for each other grew, and their security was assured for years to come. A beautiful legacy!
>
> **The Parents' Blind Spot:** Not communicating with their children about their estate plan meant that they may never have had an opportunity to co-create a multi-generation family legacy.

If communication with children about their parents' finances is rare in this culture, communication about what happens after their parents die is even rarer. Lack of communication on this issue can destroy families and lead to tragic misunderstandings, battles, and lawsuits. The absence of communication leaves children with only their imaginations, and the imaginations of grieving children often get out of control.

When our clients feel confident that their finances will support them through their lifetimes, and they have achieved a sense of clarity about the legacies they wish to leave, many of them hold family meetings with their children to discuss the disposition of their estates. These meetings can be held with only family members or, if the family feels they need extra support and guidance, they can be facilitated by a professional. The purpose is the same: to make sure that everyone is clear about the true intentions of the creator of the estate and the reasons behind certain decisions. These meetings not only provide clarity to all concerned, but may also elicit new ideas.

> Nancy and Phil had planned to leave their entire inheritance to their two children, but both children already had successful careers. Neither had an extravagant life-style and neither really wanted the money (or the exorbitant estate taxes that would be due). At their family meeting, Nancy and Phil took this into consideration and arranged to have most of the money bequeathed to a community college that would dedicate a building in the family name. Nancy and Phil were thrilled to think of how proud their grandchildren and great-grandchildren would be to walk through that campus and point to the building bearing their name.
> **Nancy and Phil's Blind Spot:** Nancy and Phil assumed that their money should be left to their children, whether they needed or wanted it.

Of course, family meetings must be age appropriate. A six-year-old will not understand or want to hear about what happens if mom or dad dies. As children mature, it can be extremely valuable to share your intentions for your legacy.

An Attitude of Gratitude and Generosity

Another quality of strong families is that they are involved in philanthropy. Gratitude and generosity are key components of a happy, satisfying life, and grateful children tend to be better stewards of wealth. How do you help your children discover the values of gratitude and generosity?

Setting a good example is a start, of course. Children who often hear their parents express gratitude verbally and see them show appreciation in small and large ways are more likely to develop similar habits and values. If parents and grandparents feel wonderful about giving to the community, to those less fortunate, to friends, and to one another, children will learn to enjoy generosity as well. Children can learn the joy of giving their time, talents, and treasures at any age. Teaching them at a young age not only establishes good habits, but it adds to their positive self-esteem.

> The Miller family started a family philanthropic project, allocating a certain amount to each family member to donate. The children are asked to identify causes for which they are passionate, then research various charities that support those causes. They look at mission statements and review the organizations' financials. The family discusses the organizations, comes to decisions about giving, and develops criteria to track the charity's progress. When possible, the family takes a field trip to visit the chosen charity or one of its projects.

Generous Kids, by Colleen O'Donnell and Lyn Baker, is an excellent resource that provides many simple ways to involve children in giving, earning, and appreciating what they have. Consider these basic ideas:

- Bring your children with you when you volunteer.
- Ask your children to donate some of their allowance money to help a cause they admire.
- Encourage your children to organize a fund drive at school for a non-profit organization they respect.
- Let your children volunteer at an animal shelter or for the Special Olympics.
- Watch movies with your children that inspire generosity and gratitude.
- Start a family tradition of giving to those in need, rather than to other family members for holidays and birthdays.
- Insist that children write thank-you notes for any gifts or acts of kindness.

There are endless ways to teach children how to help others and be appreciative of what they have. It not only prepares them to be good stewards of wealth but also helps them discover the value of making contributions, one of wealth's treasures. The values that the children in your life inherit from you will be cherished far more than the money you leave behind.

TAKING ACTION: Empowering Children

1. Write down the name of each child in your life. Think of each individually, and ask yourself what you would like to leave him or her. What value, asset, or knowledge would be most beneficial to that young person? How can you best provide it?

2. Consider what your children need to know about finance and money. How can you best teach it to them?

3. Hold a family meeting. Gather your children and begin a conversation about money and their potential inheritance. Invite a facilitator to these discussions if you feel one would be helpful.

PART **FOUR**
Contentment

CHAPTER TEN
Finding Your Contentment

Contentment (n): serenity, gladness, satisfaction, happiness, pleasure, gratification, ease

Contentment is not just an emotion, it's a state of being, a sense that all is well. What a wonderful state to be in! Of course, life has its problems and nobody is content all the time, but having moments of contentment is an indication of a life well lived. Here are some comments that we have heard from our clients that signify they are content:

These are the happiest years of our life.

I do what I want, I don't worry about money, and my family is a great source of happiness.

I'm so busy now that I'm retired, I don't know how I ever found the time to work! I choose everything I do now, and it's everything I love. I have great friends, and we do fun activities. I volunteer at the food bank and it feeds my soul. Life is good.

We were very nervous when the stock market went down. After close examination, we realized we had enough in cash and bonds to live our normal lifestyle for several years while the stock market recovers.

One of our goals is to help people have a comfortable relationship with money so that they can live a happy life. We have pondered why some people can't seem to be content with their wealth, and distilled 10 guidelines that we have found help people reach that state of contentment.

1. **Have the goal to be happy, and to really want happiness for yourself.** Too many people feel that they don't deserve happiness or that it is too far out of their reach. Abraham Lincoln said, "A person will be just about as happy as they make up their minds to be." Managing your emotions and expectations is as important as managing your money.

2. **Avoid the "comparison complex."**

   In his book, *Your Money and Your Brain*, Jason Zweig explains that people are biologically hardwired to compare themselves with others. In the U.S., there is always someone richer than you (and someone poorer, though people rarely consider that side of the equation). Without a solid focus on yourself, your own goals and wishes, and how satisfied you are with your life, you can be gripped by discontentment through comparison.

3. **Accept your financial station in life and live within its parameters.**

   Most people have stable financial circumstances at some stage in their adult lives. If your circumstances are stable and you don't plan to dramatically alter them, the wealth you've built is what you have. Contentment comes from working within your financial parameters.

4. **Satisfy your soul's purpose.**

   No matter how much you have of something, whether it is vacation homes or flashy cars, if these aren't the things you want, they will never make you happy. Getting enough of the wrong thing is never going to do the trick. Consider Clare Booth Luce's life, as mentioned in Chapter One. She married Henry Luce, editor of *Time*, *Fortune*, *Life*, and *Sports Illustrated* magazines, and was a war correspondent, a U.S. congresswoman, and ambassador to Italy—an exciting, successful woman by any measure. But all she really wanted to do was write.

5. **Develop an attitude of gratitude.**

   The happiest people seem to be those who look at life as one big blessing and see daily occurrences as synchronicities meant to benefit them. This attitude has been defined as "benevolent paranoia," the overwhelming sense that the world is plotting for your well-being. Gratitude doesn't come naturally to everyone, so some people keep a daily gratitude journal, noting five things they were grateful for during the day, to help focus on the good things in their lives. Like building up muscle, the practice of gratitude enhances the attitude of gratitude.

6. **Put consumerism in its proper place.**

   The western economy is built on a culture of consumerism. Consumerism surrounds your daily life, in conversations with friends and in the media. The idea that people know their own likes and dislikes is a basic principle of economics, but how many times have you bought something only to realize later that you never really wanted it in the first place? New clothes, with their price tags still on, may hang in your closet for months, and second homes may sit empty much more than you imagined they would. Oscar Wilde might have been describing peoples' infatuation with consumer goods when he wrote, "In this world there are only two tragedies. One is not getting what one wants, and the other is getting it." Think carefully about your real desires before you make empty purchases.

7. **Be connected with other people.**
   As we discussed in Part One, the foremost source of happiness is not money, even though that's what most people answer when they are asked what would improve the quality of their lives. Psychologists Ed Diener and Martin Seligman studied more than 200 people, administering numerous tests to determine who was genuinely happy. Their major finding was that happy people had more friends and spent less time alone than those who were unhappy.[1]

8. **Know that money is a means, and not an end.**
   Ed Diener also found that pursuing wealth for it own sake has a toxic effect on happiness.[2] Staying focused on wealth's treasures—on what is really important to you—and less on wealth itself is a key to contentment. Sir John Templeton, founder of Templeton Mutual Funds, said, "Happiness comes from spiritual wealth, not material wealth."

9. **Identify your fears and find solutions for them.**
   If recurring issues are causing you stress, develop a strategy for dealing with them. If you worry about a particular event happening, figure out a plan that will help you deal with it if it does occur. Many people are concerned with their health and worry about what would happen if they or someone in their family were seriously ill or injured. Imagine scenarios just like this and develop strategies to cope with them. Set up an account for a health fund in your financial plan, or purchase long-term care insurance. Whatever your plan, your objective is to allay your fears so they don't disrupt your sense of well-being and contentment.

10. **Maximize your sense of self-worth by devoting your time and energy to an idea, a cause, or a community that inspires you.**

    Making a difference in other people's lives, contributing your talents to the betterment of others, or helping people in need are not activities you should do to prove that you are a good person. Instead, they should inspire and motivate you. Volunteering adds meaning and satisfaction to your life that no amount of money can buy. To discover the theory behind this, you may want to read Stephen Post and Jill Neimark's book, *Why Good Things Happen to Good People: How to Live a Longer, Healthier, Happier Life by the Simple Act of Giving.*

    Contentment is not the fulfillment of what you want, but the realization of how much you already have.

    UNKNOWN

CHAPTER ELEVEN

Discovering Your Treasures

It's never just about your money—it's the treasures of wealth that we all seek.

We hope you have seen a bit of yourself in these pages: your issues, your triumphs, your desires, your fears. Through the stories of our clients, we hope that

- you'll realize that all the treasures of wealth—Clarity, Confidence, Contribution, and Contentment—are attainable and sustainable;
- you'll make your relationship with money more fulfilling, fun, and exciting; and
- you'll rediscover some dreams and visions that energize you, maybe even your purpose or mission for this life.

Now is the time for action. Throughout the book and in Appendices A through F, we've outlined questions to answer, information to gather, and steps to take. Follow the Wealth and Beyond steps in order:

1. Begin with the discovery process.
2. Determine your Red Dot.
3. Define your Strategy Filter.
4. Create your Fulfillment Plan.
5. Examine your progress by revisiting your vision and goals on a regular basis using the On-Track Monitor.

You may want to attempt these steps on your own, or you can engage professional advisors to help you with some of them. The process may seem challenging, but our clients have experienced the deep satisfaction this process brought them, and they reported that the effort was well worth it.

We wish you much success in discovering your treasures of wealth, and we'd like to leave you with one last thought:

If one advances confidently in the direction of his dreams, and endeavors to live the life which he has imagined, he will meet with a success unexpected in common hours.

HENRY DAVID THOREAU, PHILOSOPHER

APPENDICES

Creating Your Vision Statement

Following the instructions below, define and prioritize the core values that are important to you, and set goals that reflect those values. List your values and goals in a Vision Statement (a sample Vision Statement is provided). Share your statement with your advisors so they understand your vision, values, and goals and provide you with the support needed to achieve them.

Values*

By defining your values and incorporating them into your plans, you live your life according to what is most important to *you*—not what's most important to your neighbors or friends. Stating your values clearly helps you avoid the trap of pursuing money for its own sake, and allows you to use money as a tool that will empower you to enjoy what is really important to you. Money is the tool that is used to support your values.

Personal values are not the same as personal goals. Goals are the results that you seek. They require action, resources, and perhaps money. They can be checked off a list when accomplished. Personal values are the intangible qualities that make the pursuit of your goals important and meaningful to you. Understanding your unique values will help you create powerful and significant financial plans and strategies. Because you have defined the *whys* of your life, you will be motivated to follow your plans and strategies. All of your choices will move you in the same direction—the direction *you* have chosen. You have created a vision and purpose for your life and you want to capture all the possibilities you see.

---

*To help you understand the importance of values, read Jim Stovall's best-selling book *The Ultimate Gift*, or watch the movie by the same name.

Here are three suggestions to help you determine your unique values.

1. Write your biography. When you review your life experiences, you will recognize the values that were the basis of your actions, good and bad experiences, and life choices. After you have completed your biography, review it objectively to see what values emerge from the lessons you've learned. If you find talking about yourself easier than writing about yourself, you can use a recorder to dictate your biography. You will then be able to listen to yourself or have it transcribed so you can review your thoughts in a written format. The point is to use whatever method you are most comfortable with. This exercise helps you see all the most important experiences of your lifetime. You may need to have someone else help you, such as a friend, family member, advisor, or even a personal historian—someone who writes personal biographies for a living. Visit www.personalhistorians.org to find a personal historian.

2. Review the list of basic values below and circle the ones that are important to you. After you've circled all the values that attract you, trim the list down to your top 10. Next, on the worksheet that follows, rank your values from 1 to 10. Beside each value, note the experience in your life that made it important to you. Feel free to add values that are not listed here. By looking at the list and your experiences, you should come to see some common threads relating to you and your values. Summarizing your results will give you a more realistic picture of who you are and what is most important to you.

Basic Values

Circle all the values that are important to you.

Accomplishment	Financial security	Prosperity, wealth
Adventure	Freedom	Recognition
Beauty	Friendship	Recreation
Caring	Fun	Religion
Comfort	Generosity	Responsibility
Commitment	Gratitude	Results
Communication	Health	Romance
Community	Helping others	Security
Compassion	Independence	Self expression
Competition	Innovation	Simplicity
Connection	Integrity	Spirituality
Creativity	Justice	Team work
Dependability	Knowledge	Thrift
Discipline	Leadership	Tolerance
Education	Love	Tradition
Environment	Making a difference	Truth
Excellence	Patriotism	Well being
Exploration	Peace	Wisdom
Fairness	Personal growth	Work
Family	Power, influence	

Values Worksheet

Prioritize your top 10 values below. Next to each value, note the life experience that contributed to making it important to you.

	Value	What happened in my life that makes this important to me
1		
2		
3		
4		
5		

	Value	What happened in my life that makes this important to me
6		
7		
8		
9		
10		

3. Have a "values conversation" with a partner. We have used this conversation with many of our clients and witnessed its effectiveness first hand. Going through this simple but in-depth process with a partner will help reveal your core personal values and prioritize your goals. All you need is a pen or pencil, paper, a partner, and the right attitude: one of curiosity, honesty, openness, and willingness to discover what makes life meaningful to you. Also, reading Bill Bachrach's book, *Values-Based Financial Planning*, can help you with this step.

Here is how the values conversation works:

1. Your partner asks you a simple question: "What is important about money to you?"
2. Answer truthfully and from your heart. Take as much time as you need, but give the first answer that comes to mind.
3. Your partner records your answer at the bottom of the paper.
4. Then your partner builds on your answer by asking another question: "What is important about (your previous answer) to you?"
5. Again, you respond with your first thought and your partner records your answer just above your previous answer, then asks you the question once more: "What is important about (your previous answer) to you?"
6. Continue in this manner, with your partner recording your answers one above the other until you have exhausted your possibilities and can go no further.

When asking the questions, your partner should emphasize the words "to you," because money, like values, means different things to different people. Some pursue wealth for security, others for freedom, and others for something entirely different. This conversation should help you uncover your true and deepest values. Consider the emotional power of values such as independence, pride, providing for your family, achievement, balance, making a difference, fulfillment, inner peace, and self-worth. These are only a few examples of the values you may uncover as ones that are really important to you.

Following is a sample of the "values staircase" that the exercise will produce, showing the results.

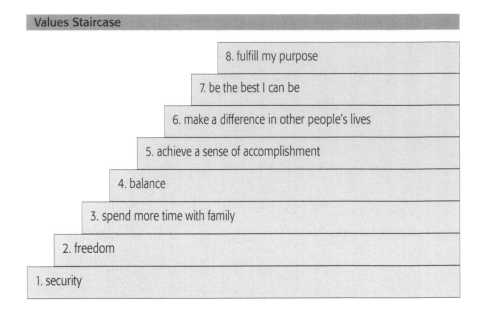

Values Staircase

8. fulfill my purpose

7. be the best I can be

6. make a difference in other people's lives

5. achieve a sense of accomplishment

4. balance

3. spend more time with family

2. freedom

1. security

Your core values may comprise a completely different list. Of course, there are no wrong answers—your answers are right for *you*.

The greatest connection between your values and your financial future is at the highest level of the values staircase. People tend to arrive at their ultimate answer after answering the values question seven to nine times. Regardless of the number of answers, every complete values conversation tends to move through three levels:

1. **Level One responses** come from your basic personal concerns about money, material goods, security, and freedom. These basic concerns are about taking care of your fundamental needs and receiving the immediate payoffs of wealth.
2. **Level Two responses** are more thoughtful, and usually related to other people and to social consciousness: providing for your family, having an impact on the community, and making a difference in the world.
3. **Level Three responses** focus on the "inner self." The values tend to be related to spiritual fulfillment: accomplishing your destiny or purpose, becoming the best person you can be, and finding inner peace or enlightenment.

People usually have several answers at each level, and sometimes people bounce up and down a level in the course of the conversation. At the third level, you gain a sense of your real purpose or mission in life, and you can reflect on the impact your financial choices will have on your values. For more information, read *Values-Based Financial Planning* by Bill Bachrach (www.bachrachvbs.com).

Once you are aware of your values, you can begin to set goals that are truly appropriate for you.

Goal Setting

Now that you know what values are important to you, you can answer goal-related questions, such as "What do I want to be doing in one year, three years, five years, ten years, and before I die?" Review and set goals as they relate to every aspect of your life: financial, physical, spiritual, emotional, intellectual, professional, recreational, familial, social, and communal.

Unlike intangible values, goals should be tangible and concrete. The best goals are SMART—specific, measurable, attainable, realistic, and time-bound. To read more about the SMART goal-setting method, visit topachievement.com/smart.

Sample Vision Statement

My vision is

- to use our money to enhance our lifestyle during our active years and secure our lifestyle during our sedentary years
- to have our money enrich ourselves, our family, and our community

My values are

- to focus on ways to enhance our love for each other and for our family and friends
- to make a difference in the lives of others and in our community by contributing time and money
- to support education and self-reliance as values we want our children and grandchildren to inherit
- to act with integrity and kindness to all we come into contact with

My wealth priorities are

- peace of mind
- more income for us
- more free time for us to enjoy life
- a substantial inheritance for our children and grandchildren
- turning our tax dollars into charitable dollars

My goals are

- to take a trip around the world
- to visit our grandchildren every three months
- to buy a new car every six years
- to receive $150,000 annually for our lifestyle
- to hire advisors to free us from money management tasks
- to update our estate plan—give $1,000,000 to each of our three children
- to give $160,000 to each of our 10 grandchildren for college
- to have a zero-tax estate plan (no income or estate taxes)
- to create a charitable legacy for our three favorite charities

Creating the Red Dot™

Fill out the form that follows to create your complete net worth summary as part of the Red Dot process. Most people are able to fill this out themselves; it's just a matter of putting the time aside to do it. However, some people find that using a financial professional to help them fill it out or to complete it for them ensures that they will actually follow through on it.

The net worth statement that follows is broken down into several sections:

* Personal assets—both liquid and illiquid
* Tax-deferred assets—all types of retirement plans and annuities
* Use assets—assets that you don't plan to use for retirement income
* Liabilities—all the money you have borrowed

If there are assets you want to evaluate more thoroughly, fill out the Asset Microscope form as well.

This net worth statement differs from a normal net worth statement because

* it includes names of institutions and account numbers so that you can also use it as a Schedule A in your estate plan;
* it notes titles on assets such as community property, joint tenancy, living trusts, and specific types of trusts;
* it lists the beneficiaries of all retirement accounts and life insurance policies;
* it lists the cost basis information for each personal asset so that you can quickly consider the tax consequences of a sale opportunity; and
* it details your liabilities, so you can easily consider refinancing or repayment.

Red Dot™ Net Worth Statement

Personal net worth for: _____   Date: _____

ASSETS

Investment Assets–Personal	Institution	Account #	Current Value	Title	Cost Basis
Liquid Assets					
Cash–Checking					
Cash–Money Market					
Cash–Savings					
CDs					
Brokerage Accounts					
Mutual Funds					
Bonds–Tax-Free, Other					
Stocks					
Cash Value–Life Insurance					
Total Liquid Assets			$		

Investment Assets–Personal	Institution	Account #	Current Value	Title	Cost Basis
Illiquid Assets					
Real Estate (Market Value)					
Ltd Partnerships, LLC Interests					
Notes, Deeds of Trust					
Other					
Total Illiquid Assets			$		
Total Personal Assets			$		

Investment Assets— Tax-Deferred	Institution	Account #	Current Value	Owner	Beneficiary Designation	
					Primary	**Contingent**
Retirement Plans						
401k, 403(b), Other						
IRAs, SEP IRA						
Roth IRA						
Annuities–Qualified						
Annuities–Non-Qualified			*	*		
Total Tax-Deferred Assets			$			
Total Investment Assets			$			

*Title/Cost Basis

Use Assets		Current Value	Title	
Home				
Vacation Home				
Vehicles, Boat, Other				
Art, Jewelry, Collections, etc.				
Total Use Assets		$		
Total Assets		$		

Liabilities	Institution	Account #	Current Value	%	Maturity Date
Home Mortgage					
Real Estate Loans					
Car Loans					
Credit Cards, Loans					
Equity Line of Credit					
Total Liabilities			$		

	Current Value
Total Assets	
less **Total Liabilities**	
Total Net Worth	$

	Face Amount	Beneficiary Designation	
		Primary	**Contingent**
Life Insurance			
Total Estate Net Worth	$		

Asset Microscope™

Name: _____ Date: _____

Type of asset: _____

Market value: $_____ Ownership: _____ %

Title of ownership: _____

Date of acquisition: _____

Original debt amount: $_____ Current debt amount: $_____

Interest rate: _____% Term: _____ Cost basis: $_____

Purpose of this investment (*the reasoning behind the decision to make the investment*):

_____

_____

Current income: $_____ Current expenses: $_____

Future potential: _____

_____

10-year goal for this asset: _____

_____

At what point should this asset be sold? _____

_____

Should this asset be kept for a long time? ____ Yes ____ No

Why? _____

_____

_____

Should this asset be transferred to my heirs? ____ Yes ____ No

Why? _____

_____

Is this an asset to transfer from generation to generation? ___Yes ___No

Why? _____

_____

_____

Preparing Your Lifestyle Price Tag™

A Lifestyle Price Tag is different from a budget or a summary of expenses. It is a summary of what your *desired* lifestyle would cost. Many people do not want to deal with the level of detail involved in calculating their Lifestyle Price Tag, and instead choose a round figure, such as $200,000 per year. However, if their current assets won't support their ideal lifestyle, they need to determine the details of their desired spending so they can know what to adjust. We have found that often, once clients complete a financial independence and retirement projection, they become interested in the details. The details give them the peace of mind they need, confirming that their dreams can be attained with their current asset base.

When you calculate your Lifestyle Price Tag, you can use what you are spending today as a base. You may need to adjust these numbers to account for the changes that will take place over the next several years. Some examples of adjustments are listed here:

- **Expenses that will be eliminated.** For example, house payments, children's expenses, and work expenses.
- **Expenses that will increase.** For example, expenses usually paid by the business, entertainment costs (because you will have additional time to spend money), travel costs, and hobby costs.
- **An additional amount, just to be conservative.** Inflation is always factored in separately, but some people add in an extra 10 to 20 percent. They do this to give themselves the flexibility to do anything they want.
- **Uncertain expenses.** Home and car maintenance are good examples of uncertain expenses; the worksheet headed "Bills Not Paid on a Monthly Basis" lists the type of expenses that you can estimate on a quarterly, semi-annual, or annual basis.
- **Extraordinary expenses, expected or desired.** On the last worksheet, you can list time-bound extraordinary expenses such as a new roof. This

worksheet gives you the opportunity to think through the extra expenses you might have. You can also consider how much fun money you'll want, or how much money you'll need to explore new opportunities at different ages.

- **Life-stage expenses.** We talked about three distinct periods of retirement: the Go-Go Years, the Slow-Go Years, and the No-Go Years. You can add in expenses for each life stage to the extraordinary expenses worksheet. Because travel expenses will be higher in the Go-Go Years, you might add a travel fund of $25,000 a year from ages 60 to 75. In the Slow-Go or No-Go Years, you could add an estimate for unknown medical expenses. Some clients add an annual estimate to their summary or assume a lump sum cost, such as $300,000, to ensure they have enough for unknown and uncovered medical costs.

Your Lifestyle Price Tag™

Retirement Income	Monthly	Annually
Salary (net of taxes)	$	$
Pension	$	$
Interest	$	$
Dividends	$	$
Rental (net of expenses)	$	$
Social Security	$	$
Amounts from investments	$	$
Other _____	$	$
Total Income	$	$
Expenses	**Monthly**	**Annually**
Expense Worksheet totals	$	$
Total payments to creditors	$	$
Total non-monthly bills	$	$
Total Expenses	$	$
Difference	$	$

Expense Worksheet

	Monthly	Annually
Savings		
Credit union	$	$
Investments	$	$
Retirement plans	$	$
Housing		
Mortgage/rent	$	$
Maintenance	$	$
Insurance	$	$
Other _____	$	$
Utilities		
Electricity	$	$
Gas	$	$
Water	$	$
Garbage	$	$
Other _____	$	$
Telephone		
Service	$	$
Long distance	$	$
Cellular	$	$
Food		
Groceries	$	$
Lunch out	$	$
Dinner out	$	$
Other _____	$	$
Transportation		
Gas	$	$
Car maintenance	$	$
Car insurance	$	$
Parking/bus fare	$	$
Other _____	$	$

	Monthly	Annually
Clothing/Personal		
For you	$	$
For spouse	$	$
Dry cleaning	$	$
Hair care	$	$
Health club	$	$
Other _____	$	$
Child Expenses		
Day care/babysitter	$	$
Allowances	$	$
Child support	$	$
Toys/clothes	$	$
Other _____	$	$
Education		
Tuition/supplies	$	$
Lessons (music, etc.)	$	$
Other _____	$	$
Medical		
Doctor	$	$
Dentist	$	$
Optometrist	$	$
Specialist	$	$
Medication	$	$
Vitamins	$	$
Other _____	$	$
Insurance		
Life/disability	$	$
Health/dental	$	$
Entertainment		
Movies/theater	$	$
Hobbies/clubs	$	$
Sports (e.g., skiing)	$	$

	Monthly	Annually
Weekend trips	$	$
Cable/Internet	$	$
Other _____	$	$
Pet Care		
Pet food	$	$
Grooming	$	$
Kennel costs	$	$
Vet/licenses	$	$
Other _____	$	$
Miscellaneous		
Cash/pocket money	$	$
Gifts	$	$
Donations	$	$
Postage	$	$
Newspaper/magazines/books	$	$
CDs/DVDs	$	$
Other _____	$	$
Total Expenses	$	$

List of Creditors

(Bills, Loans, Debts)

Name of Creditor	Balance Owed	Monthly Payment	Interest Rate
	$	$	%
	$	$	%
	$	$	%
	$	$	%
	$	$	%
	$	$	%
	$	$	%
Creditor Totals	$	$	%

Bills Not Paid on a Monthly Basis

Fill in the amount for each item in the appropriate column.

Item	Quarterly	Semi-annually	Annually
Insurance (car/life/home)	$	$	$
Christmas/gifts	$	$	$
Investments	$	$	$
Taxes (property/income)	$	$	$
School tuition	$	$	$
Clothes	$	$	$
Vacation	$	$	$
Maintenance (home/car)	$	$	$
DMV registration	$	$	$
Medical deductible	$	$	$
Other _____	$	$	$
Total Payments	$	$	$
	× 4	× 2	
Annual Totals	$	$	$

Sum of three annual totals above:	$
Amount to save monthly to meet these expenses: **(sum divided by 12)**	$

Extraordinary Expenses–Expected or Desired

Extraordinary expenses do not figure into your Lifestyle Price Tag; they're the expenses that will come up infrequently. You have two options when considering extraordinary expenses: (1) you can set aside the capital you'll need to cover these expenses; or (2) you can save monthly to accumulate the money you'll need to cover each goal or expense.

Year	Travel	Cars	Purchases	Other
	$	$	$	$
	$	$	$	$
	$	$	$	$
	$	$	$	$
	$	$	$	$
	$	$	$	$
	$	$	$	$
	$	$	$	$
	$	$	$	$
	$	$	$	$
	$	$	$	$
	$	$	$	$

Your Financial Independence Projection

To ensure that you will be financially independent and secure for the rest of your life, we recommend that you work with a financial advisor to create a complete financial independence projection. While there are no guarantees, this kind of projection will give you an idea of how secure you are when you use your current assets for your financial independence.

Determining Your Own Projection

If you prefer to do your own projection, you'll need some meaningful assumptions to determine how long you'll need your assets for and how long they can be expected to last. You'll need to make these assumptions:

- **Life expectancy:** Normal life expectancy is approximately 78 years (75 for men, 80 for women). However, since the current trend is toward people living longer, some people assume they will live 10 years longer than their ancestors, while others run their projections to age 100, just to be sure they will always have enough money.
- **Inflation:** For the last 25 years, inflation has averaged 3 percent, so most people use this figure in their assumptions. For the last 5 years, inflation has averaged 2.5 percent, so some people prefer this more recent number.
- **Rate of return:** The assumption you use for rate of return should depend on how aggressively you invest. Conservative investors may use 3 to 4 percent, moderate investors 4 to 6 percent, and aggressive investors 6 to 8 percent. Another option is to consider the differential between inflation and rate of return as the important number. For example, if your inflation assumption is 3 percent and your rate of return assumption is 6 percent, you would need to earn 3 percent over inflation. Then, if any of the numbers change over time, you only need to focus on your portfolio getting a specific percentage over inflation.

AARP provides a retirement planning calculator on its website, www.
aarp.org, that can also assist you in doing a projection. You can find the
calculator by selecting "Money" and then "Retirement." It is the best free
calculator we've found. Most entries within the calculator are self-explanatory,
but the following entries are ones that we felt needed some clarification.

Desired Annual Household Income during Retirement

There are two possible approaches to estimating this amount:

- You can estimate your desired retirement income using your current
  salary. If you spend all the income you make now and don't expect that
  to change, your current salary would be a reasonable estimate.
- You can sum up what you spend now. See Appendix C for the worksheet
  to calculate your total expenses. Many people do one projection using
  estimates, and then do a second projection using "hard" numbers they've
  calculated to get a more precise projection.

Desired Estate

This is the amount you would like to have left over to pass on to your heirs.
Zero is a possible answer. Some people do not include their home equity as
part of their current retirement assets because they want to live in their home
until they die. If you enter zero here and do not include your home equity in
your retirement assets, your home would be the estate left to your heirs.

Current Retirement Assets

This is the total of all the assets you own that you plan to use for retirement income. Decide if you want to include the value of your house in this
number. You can include the value, not just the equity, if you plan to pay off
the mortgage. The calculator provides boxes for each partner, but for jointly
owned assets, enter the total in one box only (it doesn't matter which one).

Monthly Contributions

This is the amount you save each year, divided by 12. It could comprise your
contributions to retirement plans, savings accounts, and investment accounts.

Investment Returns

These entries give you the flexibility to use more aggressive rates early in your
retirement and more conservative rates as you age.

Your Strategy Filter™

What is the Strategy Filter?

- It integrates your vision and your goals with investment planning, tax planning, estate planning, and evolving family dynamics to produce an easy-to-manage financial structure within which you can operate effectively.
- It is a set of statements you can use to filter potential financial strategies and instruments, allowing you to identify the ones that would be best for your situation. It keeps you focused.
- It expands upon the traditional investment policy statement, which addresses investments only.

Using the gaps you identified in Chapter Five, fill out the Strategy Filter Worksheet that follows.

Strategy Filter™ Worksheet

Date: _____

Vision

_____

_____

Goals

_____

_____

_____

_____

Red Dot™–Where We Are Now?

_____

_____

_____

_____

Gaps–What's Missing?

_____

_____

_____

_____

Supporting Resources and Advisors

_____

_____

_____

_____

Strategies

_____

_____

_____

_____

Sample Strategy Filter™ Worksheet

Date: July 2008

Vision/Goals

Financial independence to maintain current lifestyle, travel extensively, and give $12,000 per year to each of our three kids

Red Dot™–Where We Are Now?

$2.5 million invested in stock and bonds, $110,000 in annual income from investments
Needed: $140,000
Lifestyle Price Tag: $120,000 + $20,000 for travel + $36,000 from assets for gifting

Gaps–What's Missing?

1. $30,000 income shortage
2. If we gift assets to our children, we will be short of our financial independence goal

Supporting Resources and Advisors

Sandy Jones, CERTIFIED FINANCIAL PLANNER™
Dick Moore, Certified Public Accountant

Strategies

Increase income: Convert growth stocks to dividend-paying stocks and municipal bonds
Gifting: Gift low-basis stocks to children at $12,000 each
Replace assets: Work an additional five years to replace assets that we need for financial independence but are gifting to children

Your Advisory Team

Few professional athletes, successful entrepreneurs, or busy politicians make it far without a team of trusted advisors to support them. Putting together a good team of advisors is not as difficult as you might imagine; in fact, you need only take two steps to assemble your team.

Step 1: Assess What You Have

Make of a list of your current advisors next to their roles on the worksheet provided. One advisor may fill multiple roles. Rate each advisor on a scale of 1 to 5 on the following traits, with 1 being bad and 5 being excellent.

- **Trust:** Do you feel that this advisor has your best interests at heart? Do you wonder if their recommendations are for their best interests or for yours?
- **Reliability:** How reliable is this advisor? Do they fulfill their promises? Do they return your calls? Do they meet deadlines?
- **Communication:** How well does this advisor communicate with you? Can you understand what they tell you? How comfortable do you feel expressing yourself to them? Are they a good listener? Do they understand what you tell them?
- **Initiative:** Does this advisor take the initiative with you? Do they make suggestions that may benefit you?
- **Expertise:** Is this advisor an expert in their field? Do they have the level of expertise that you need in your situation? Do other professionals consider them an expert?

Total the scores in each category and then determine the minimum score you will accept for any advisor.

Advisory Team Worksheet

Advisor	Name	Trust	Reliability	Communication	Initiative	Expertise	TOTAL
Legal advisor							
Estate planning lawyer							
CPA or tax preparer							
Insurance professional (life, disability, casualty)							
Investment advisor							
Financial planner							

If you feel that you need to replace an advisor, talk with the advisors you've rated highly and ask them to recommend someone to fill that role. Many advisors have strategic alliances with other professionals with whom they work regularly, and they will understand the importance of a well-connected team.

Step 2: Assemble Your Team

Assemble a team of advisors who help you with your unique issues. For example, your team should be able to provide you with the information you need to determine whether you should sell your real estate or consider a tax-free exchange. Your real estate professional will have all the information about the transaction, your tax preparer will have the accurate capital gains information and the tax perspective, and your financial planner should have all the information about your goals, current income needs, and income and growth requirements for achieving financial independence.

Some of your advisors may be able to fill multiple roles. For example, financial planners work with clients over many years, so they may be able to help them in other areas. When a client needs to do estate planning, some financial planners have a wealth of relevant information that can facilitate the estate planning process. They should have their client's net worth statement, account numbers, account titles, and names of retirement plan beneficiaries. They may also know the family history and understand the family dynamics and any possible problem areas.

A big advancement in building advisor teams is the concept of the team leader, wealth coach, or lead advisor. This person knows your big picture: your vision, values, and short- and long-term goals. They have all the details regarding your financial picture, including

- your net worth statement and Asset Microscope;
- your financial independence status;
- your Lifestyle Price Tag and your sources of income;
- your tax returns;
- your estate and legacy plan;
- your insurance information;
- your investment details; and
- the names and contact information of your other advisors.

When there is a project to implement or a new strategy to consider, your team leader

- ensures that the strategy or project is compatible with your mission, vision, values, and goals;
- discusses technical details with your team to save you the trouble of having to sit through discussions that could increase your advisor costs or take you away from what you'd prefer to be doing;
- presents you with the decision that your advisors have determined is best; and
- ensures that your needed actions get completed.

Many people don't realize that if they don't hire a team leader, they must fill that role themselves, but they are often unaware of all the details needing attention in order to complete a project. A wealth coach or lead advisor can ensure that what you start is completed without requiring your constant attention.

Interview your existing team members to see who is available to be your team leader. If no one on your team can do it, consider finding an outside source who would be appropriate.

Team Leader Resources

Wealth Coaches: The Legacy Companies has a network of wealth coaches. Go to their website, www.legacyboston.com, and look for The Legacy Wealth Coach Network under "Programs."

Personal CFO: You may find companies that provide personal CFOs by searching for "personal CFO" via a search engine like Google.

Institute of Certified Financial Planners (ICFP) and National Association of Personal Financial Advisors (NAPFA): Some of the advisors who belong to these organizations are focused on the type of holistic planning discussed in this book. Interview association members to determine what levels of planning they do and to ensure they aren't just in the business of selling products. Be sure they are interested in going through an in-depth discovery process with you, not just goal setting.

Advisors in Philanthropy: This is a network of professional advisors who are devoted to mastering and promoting the principles and practices of client-centered planning. Their website is www.advisorsinphilanthropy.org.

References and Resources

References

Part One: Clarity

Chapter One: *Creating Wealth* versus *Creating Happiness*

[1] Zweig, Jason. 2007. *Your Money and Your Brain: How the New Science of Neuroeconomics Can Help Make You Rich.* New York: Simon & Schuster.

[2] *Ibid.*

[3] Veenhoven, Ruut. *World Database of Happiness.* Erasmus University Rotterdam. worlddatabaseofhappiness.eur.nl.

[4] Easterbrook, Gregg. 2005. The Real Truth about Money. *Time* 165(3)32–34.

[5] Chatzky, Jean. 2003. 10 Commandments of Financial Happiness. *Money* 32(10)113.

[6] Zweig. 2007. *Your Money and Your Brain.*

[7] Schervish, Paul G. and Havens, John J. 1999. *Millionaires and the Millennium: New Estimates of the Forthcoming Wealth Transfer and the Prospects for a Golden Age of Philanthropy.* Boston College Center on Wealth and Philanthropy.

[8] Morris, Sylvia. 1997. *Rage for Fame: The Ascent of Clare Boothe Luce.* New York: Random House.

Part Two: Confidence

Chapter Four: Step Two—Your Red Dot™

[1] Schervish and Havens. 1999. *Millionaires and the Millennium.*

Part Three: Contribution

Chapter Eight: Legacy Planning

[1] *More Than Money Magazine.* Issue Number 42, December 2005.

Chapter Nine: Empowering Children

[1] Schervish and Havens. 1999. *Millionaires and the Millennium.*

[2] Prince, Russ Alan and Schiff, Lewis. 2006. *The Influence of Affluence: How the New Rich Are Changing America.* New York: Broadway Books.

Part Four: Contentment

Chapter Ten: Finding Your Contentment

[1] Diener, Ed and Seligman, Martin E.P. 2002. Very Happy People. *Psychological Science* 13(1)81–84.

[2] Diener, Ed and Biswas-Diener, Robert. 2002. Will Money Increase Subjective Well-Being? *Social Indicators Research* 57(2002)119–169.

Recommended Resources

Books

Bachrach, Bill. 2000. *Values-Based Financial Planning: The Art of Creating an Inspiring Financial Strategy.* www.bachrachvbs.com.

Fithian, Scott C. 2000. *Values-Based Estate Planning: A Step-by-Step Approach to Wealth Transfer for Professional Advisors.* New York: John Wiley & Sons, Inc.

Hughes, James E. Jr. 2004. *Family Wealth—Keeping It in the Family: How Family Members and Their Advisers Preserve Human, Intellectual, and Financial Assets for Generations.* Princeton, NJ: Bloomberg Press.

Kline, Nancy. 1998. *Time to Think: Listening to Ignite the Human Mind.* London: Cassell Illustrated.

O'Donnell, Colleen and Baker, Lyn. 2007. *Generous Kids: Helping Your Child Experience the Joy of Giving.* Dallas: Brown Books Publishing Group.

Ottinger, Randall J. 2008. *Beyond Success: Building a Personal, Financial, and Philanthropic Legacy*. New York: McGraw-Hill.

Post, Stephen and Neimark, Jill. 2007. *Why Good Things Happen to Good People: How to Live a Longer, Healthier, Happier Life by the Simple Act of Giving*. New York: Broadway Books.

Rose, Tony. 2008. *Say Hello to the Elephants*. Encino, CA: RSJ Swenson LLC.

Stovall, Jim. 2007. *The Ultimate Gift*. Colorado Springs: David C. Cook.

Willis, Thayer Cheatham. 2003. *Navigating the Dark Side of Wealth: A Life Guide for Inheritors*. Portland, OR: New Concord Press.

Zweig, Jason. 2007. *Your Money and Your Brain: How the New Science of Neuroeconomics Can Help Make You Rich*. New York: Simon & Schuster.

Websites

AARP: www.aarp.org

Advisors in Philanthropy: www.advisorsinphilanthropy.org

Association of Personal Historians: www.personalhistorians.org

Boston College Center on Wealth and Philanthropy: www.bc.edu/research/cwp

Foord Van Bruggen Ebersole & Pajak Financial Services: www.wealthandbeyondprogram.com

Institute of Certified Financial Planners: www.cfp.net

The Legacy Wealth Coach Network: www.legacyboston.com

National Association of Personal Financial Advisors: www.napfa.org

NOTES